PREDICTING ADOLESCENT DRUG USE

PREDICTING ADOLESCENT DRUG USE

Utility Structure and Marijuana

Karl E. Bauman

PRAEGER

PRAEGER SPECIAL STUDIES • PRAEGER SCIENTIFIC

Library of Congress Cataloging in Publication Data

Bauman, Karl E
   Predicting adolescent drug use.

   Includes bibliographies and index.
   1. Drugs and youth--United States.
2. Drug abuse, Prediction of--United States.
I. Title.
HV5824.Y68B38   362.7'8'2930973   79-22736
ISBN 0-03-050636-0

Published in 1980 by Praeger Publishers
CBS Educational and Professional Publishing
A Division of CBS, Inc.
521 Fifth Avenue, New York, New York 10017 U.S.A.

© 1980 by Praeger Publishers

0123456789   038   987654321

Printed in the United States of America

PREFACE

Nature has placed mankind under the governance of
two sovereign masters, pain and pleasure. It is
for them alone . . . to determine what we shall do.
(Bentham, 1780)*

The realization that pain and pleasure are central to understanding behavior has been postulated in various forms before and
since Jeremy Bentham's classic statement in 1780. If the postulate
is true, then it explains why people behave as they do, an understanding sought by philosophers, behavioral scientists, and others
through careers and centuries. The purpose of this book is to summarize the author's research incorporating the pleasure-pain principle as a central premise within a utility model and applying it to
the explanation of behavior with marijuana among adolescents.

The first chapter describes the utility theory as formulated
for this study, relates this version of the theory to earlier research, and offers reasons for considering the study to be of particular significance. Chapter 2 outlines the general strategy chosen
to test the hypotheses that were derived from the theory, describes
the research locale, and presents the questionnaire used for collecting data. Chapter 3 summarizes the data collection procedures,
and Chapter 4 describes the sample. The findings are presented in
Chapters 5 through 10. The final chapter discusses the implications of the study for future research, programs and policy, and
choice behavior.

---

*By permission of Basil Blackwood, Oxford.

ACKNOWLEDGMENTS

Many people contributed to the research reported in this book. First and foremost are the young people who provided the necessary data, and their parents who gave them permission to participate. While making this research possible, the positive interactions with them and their encouragement helped make this a most enjoyable endeavor. The author is also indebted to the Chapel Hill-Carrboro city schools for collaborating on our pilot studies, and to the Wake County schools for serving as the primary research locale. Mr. Wayne Bare of the Wake County schools receives our special thanks for providing insight and understanding throughout the study.

Among colleagues whose ideas and actions contributed to this research are Elizabeth Bryan, Becky James, Gary Koch, Elisabeth Sage, Richard Shachtman, and Paul Thompson, and to them many of the positive features of this study are attributed.

Several organizations of the University of North Carolina at Chapel Hill facilitated the research. The author is especially grateful to the Department of Maternal and Child Health, the Office of the Dean of the School of Public Health, the Computer Data and Processing Facility of the School of Public Health, and the Institute for Research in Social Science. The support they provided was frequent and essential.

The School of Public Health and the National Institutes of Health provided a General Research Support grant to plan this research. That grant yielded a formal application for funding the study and the award of Grant Number 1 R01 DA01127 from the National Institute on Drug Abuse of the U.S. Department of Health, Education and Welfare. The contribution to this research by these grantors was substantial.

CONTENTS

1
A VERSION OF UTILITY THEORY

This chapter begins by defining the utility structure, and by placing this variable within a framework for considering behavior with marijuana. The formulation is related to earlier research, and reasons are given for considering it important to test the hypotheses derived from the theory.

DEFINITION OF THE UTILITY STRUCTURE

The utility structure is the variable of central focus in this study. As conceptualized, this variable has five interrelated components: anticipated consequences (or attributes), salience, subjective probability, delayed consequence, and time orientation.

Anticipated Consequences

People anticipate positive and negative consequences of behavior. The central hypothesis from utility theory is that the imbalance of these positive and negative consequences determines behavior. If an individual's positive consequences outweigh the negative consequences, then the individual will behave in one way; whereas if the individual's negative consequences outweigh the positive consequences, then the individual will behave in another way. This derives from the basic principle of many theories of human behavior that behavior results from the attempt to maximize favorable experiences and minimize unfavorable experiences, that people act to experience pleasure and to avoid pain.

Many explanations for people's use or nonuse of marijuana can be classified as anticipated consequences. Some people are said to use marijuana because they expect good consequences, such

1

as relief from tension, approval by peers, and a good time. Some people do not use marijuana because they anticipate bad outcomes, such as nausea, reprimand from others, and addiction. It is predicted that marijuana is more likely to be used if the positive consequences outweigh the negative consequences, than if the negative consequences outweigh the positive consequences. A list of selected outcomes of marijuana is given in Table 1.1. The concepts of anticipated consequences and attributes are used interchangeably when referring to the expected outcomes of behavior.

It should be emphasized at the outset that anticipated consequences of behavior are being considered here and not necessarily actual outcomes. What the individual thinks might happen rather than what actually occurs is of concern to this version of utility theory.

Salience

It is recognized that people attach different degrees of importance (salience) to the same anticipated outcomes of behavior. For example, two individuals might believe they would receive approval from their peers if they used marijuana. However, if one considered peer approval of prime importance, whereas the other considered it of moderate importance, then the anticipated consequence of peer approval would be more significant for the first than the second individual, and when considered with other anticipated outcomes this should influence their drug behavior accordingly. Or, two individuals might perceive apprehension by the police as a consequence of using marijuana. If the first individual considers police apprehension the worst event imaginable, whereas the other does not consider that consequence to be extremely undesirable, then that anticipated consequence would carry more weight for the behavior of the first than the second individual. Moreover, a person might ascribe different degrees of salience among attributes. A person might consider peer approval and relief from anxiety very important to acquire, and enhanced courage and creativity much less important to experience. Or, being arrested by the police might be a more salient attribute than being reprimanded by parents. Thus, salience is presumed to vary by people and by attribute. Utility theorists sometimes refer to the salience of attributes as utility.

Subjective Probability

Subjective probability is an individual's perception of the likelihood that a consequence will occur as a result of behavior.

TABLE 1.1

Anticipated Positive Consequences of Marijuana

Increased
  Relaxation
  Sex drive
  Sociability
  Sensory awareness
  Interest in school work
  Interest in life
  Courage
  Self-awareness
  Friendliness
  Strength
  Sexual desires
  Intelligence
  Memory
  Recall
  Learning
  Kicks
  Thrills
  Fun
  Energy
  Creativity
  Power
  Self-confrontation
  Appetite
  Weight

Decreased
  Depression
  Tension
  Sex drive
  Nervousness
  Hostility
  Boredom
  Anger
  Irritability
  Weight
  Appetite
  Sluggishness
  Worries
  Self-consciousness
  Concern about future
  Concern about present problems
  Pressures

  Physical pain
  Psychological pain
  Inhibitions about sex
  Frustration

More satisfactory
  Sexual relations
  Relationships with others
  Mood
  Health
  Expression of anger
  Self-concept
  School performance

Additional benefits
  Escape from problems
  Pleasure
  Heightened senses
  Exhilaration
  Satisfaction of curiosity
  More out of life
  Keeping awake
  Sleep
  Pass time more quickly
  Pass time more slowly
  Ability to work beyond capacity
  Approval from friends
  Religious experience
  Getting through a crisis situation
  A good time
  Behaving like a grown-up
  Unusual thoughts
  Hallucinations
  Mystical experience
  Getting up for something, such as
    an exam or athletic event
  Attention from peers
  Attention from adults
  Getting back at parents
  Response to a dare
  Self-analysis and introspection
  Belonging with peers
  Escape from societal values
  Pleasant taste

(continued)

Table 1.1 continued

Anticipated Negative Consequences of Marijuana

Decreased
  Control over self
  Interest in school work
  Interest in other things
  Appetite
  Weight
  Length of life
  Love from others
  Love for others
  Lifetime goals
  Reputation
  Sexual desires
  Sexual drive
  Sociability
  Sensory awareness
  Courage
  Self-awareness
  Friendliness
  Strength
  Intelligence
  Memory
  Recall
  Learning
  Energy
  Creativity
  Power
  Coordination

Increased
  Depression
  Tension
  Sex drive
  Nervousness
  Hostility
  Boredom
  Anger
  Irritability
  Weight
  Appetite
  Sluggishness
  Worries
  Self-consciousness
  Concern about future
  Concern about present problems
  Pressures
  Physical pain
  Psychological pain
  Inhibitions about sex
  Frustration
  Susceptibility to disease

Less satisfactory
  Sexual relations
  Relationships with others
  Mood
  Health
  Expression of anger
  Self-concept
  School performance
  Mental stability
  Communication
  Fulfillment of responsibility

Additional drawbacks
  Legal arrest and punishment
  Financing use of drugs
  Addiction
  Disapproval by friends, adults, others
  Brain damage
  Nausea
  Bad example for others
  Deviation from values
  Vomit
  Pass time more quickly, more slowly
  Confusion
  Paranoia
  Sadness
  Unusual thoughts, scary thoughts
  Hallucinations
  Panic
  Offspring with birth defects
  Death
  Impure overdose
  Continued trips with new dose
  Headache
  Suicide
  Becoming a criminal
  Causing an accident when under
    influence
  Violence
  Hurt parents, friends
  Cost to society
  Becoming irresponsible
  Unpleasant taste
  Impotence
  Dizziness
  Shortness of breath
  Restlessness
  Convulsion
  Blindness
  Loss of consciousness

Individuals associate different subjective probabilities with the same anticipated consequences, and that may lead to a difference in behavior. For example, one individual may perceive a 25 percent probability of causing an automobile accident while under the influence of marijuana, whereas another may perceive a 75 percent probability for that consequence. Both individuals perceive causing an automobile accident as a negative outcome, but the behavior of the individual with relatively high subjective probability will presumably be influenced more by that attribute than will the behavior of an individual with the lower subjective probability for the same attribute. Moreover, subjective probability varies by attribute. For example, a person might assign a 65 percent subjective probability to nausea and a 5 percent probability to being apprehended by the police. Thus, nausea might be more influential than police apprehension upon the decision not to use marijuana, unless, of course, the difference in salience assigned these consequences offsets the difference in subjective probability. Utility theorists often call utilities that are adjusted for subjective probability "subjective expected utilities."

Delayed Consequence

The concept of delayed consequence recognizes that some consequences of behavior are expected to occur sooner after the behavior than others. Losing complete control over self while under the influence of marijuana will be perceived to be a much more immediate consequence than becoming an addict or dying from a disease caused by marijuana. Thus, whereas these more distant consequences may have higher salience to the individual than the more immediate outcome of losing control over self, the influence of salience upon behavior may be diminished by the fact that the consequences will be delayed until a long time after the behavior. Consideration of marijuana behavior in the context of utility theory takes delayed consequences into account.

Time Orientation

Time orientation recognizes that individuals vary with respect to their orientation to the present and the future. Some people are concerned only with what might happen today, whereas others are more concerned about ten years from today. Consequences to be accrued in the future will presumably make a greater contribution to the behavior of the future-oriented individual than to the person who is more oriented toward the present. For example, two individuals might perceive reduced longevity as a negative consequence of marijuana. That anticipated consequence might be extremely influential upon the future-oriented person but of minimal importance for the individual who is concerned with the present only. Since individuals are not identical with respect to time orientation, it is included as a component in the utility structure.

Recapitulation

To summarize the formulation thus far, people are viewed as having perceptions about the good and bad things that may happen to them if they use marijuana. Important components of these positive and negative consequences, which vary by people and consequence, are salience, subjective probability, delayed consequence, and time orientation. When taking these components into account the utility structure is the difference between the positive and negative attributes. The more positive the utility structure, the more likely it is that marijuana will be used, and the more negative the utility structure, the less likely that marijuana will be used.

TYPES OF MARIJUANA BEHAVIOR

The utility structure can be applied in order to understand why people ever use marijuana, why it is used as frequently as it is, whether use continues over a long or short period of time, and why use creates problems for self and others. When considering the "ever use" dependent variable, the utility structures of those who have never used marijuana can be used to predict who will use that drug in the future. In addition, among those who do use marijuana, the more positive their utility structure the greater the frequency of that behavior, whereas the more negative the utility structure the less frequently that behavior occurs. The formulation suggests that behavior will continue as long as the positive outweighs the negative and that behavior will discontinue when the negative begins outweighing the positive. Frequent and continuous behavior, determined by the utility structure, can lead to problem consumption of marijuana for self and society if the positive structure does not redistribute in favor of the more negative portion of the scale.

RECIPROCITY OF VARIABLES

It seems plausible that, in addition to the influence of the utility structure on behavior, behavior with marijuana can influence the utility structure. As the individual accumulates, through experience, information about the actual consequences of behavior, the utility structure may change and this in turn could influence behavior. Prior to consumption, a person might not identify police apprehension, nausea, and tension relief as consequences of marijuana. Or if these attributes were identified, they might not be accorded a high degree of salience or subjective probability until after consumption. This new experience would enter the utility structure and then influence behavior.

ANTECEDENT VARIABLES

Many variables commonly considered determinants of marijuana behavior can be readily classified as positive or negative consequences of marijuana, as suggested by the list in Table 1.1. Some variables cannot be classified so easily. For example, peer use, parental permissiveness, emotional stability, boredom, and availability are among the variables related to behavior with marijuana, but they cannot be considered anticipated positive or negative outcomes of behavior. A more inclusive list of such variables, considered in the present study to be antecedent to the utility structure, is presented in Table 1.2.

TABLE 1.2

Selected Antecedent Variables

Anxiety
Psychological stress
Alienation
Rebelliousness
Boredom
Availability
Curiosity
Use by peers
Use by parents
Parental permissiveness
Socioeconomic status of parents
Religiosity and religious affiliation
Place of residence
Intelligence
Conservatism

Several examples of the role of antecedent variables are given below. The degree to which parents are permissive regarding a child's behavior has been offered as an explanation for use of marijuana. Permissiveness is believed to increase the chances that the child will use marijuana, whereas restrictiveness decreases the probability of its use. Why does this occur? Perhaps the degree of permissiveness influences the utility structure and this in turn has an impact upon behavior. For example, children of permissive parents may not perceive such negative consequences of marijuana use as reprimand from parents or guilt, or the saliences or subjective probabilities associated with these consequences may be lower than for children of restrictive parents. Therefore, children of permissive parents are toward the positive end of the utility structure, indicating marijuana use by children of permissive parents and abstinence among children of restrictive parents.

Two more examples of the place of antecedent variables in the present version of the theory are as follows. Anxiety has been found to be related to use of marijuana. Perhaps people with high anxiety are more likely than those with less anxiety to expect relief from anxiety from marijuana, or that attribute is much more salient for those with high anxiety than for people with low anxiety. Thus, anxiety influences behavior through its influence upon the utility structure. Availability of marijuana is often given as the explanation for its use. When marijuana is readily available, why do some consume it and others abstain, or some use it regularly while others use it rarely? The framework of this study says that the utility structure determines whether availability results in behavior. Specifically, if the utility structure is skewed toward the positive, then marijuana will be used. If, on the other hand, the structure for the individual tends toward the negative, either drug use will not occur or it will occur infrequently, even if marijuana is available. Many more examples could be offered. Suffice it to say that variables that cannot be viewed as anticipated consequences are considered to be antecedent to, or conditioned by, the utility structure.

A theoretical scheme, including the antecedent variables, the utility structure, and behavior with marijuana, is shown in Figure 1.1, indicating that antecedent variables lead to the formation of the utility structure that influences behavior with marijuana. Moreover, marijuana behavior has a reciprocal influence on the utility structure. An arrow points back from the behavior-with-marijuana variable to the antecedent variables because marijuana may be one of many things that influence some social and psychological attributes of individuals. That is, some of the antecedent variables can be considered consequent as well as antecedent to use of marijuana; for example, use of marijuana might influence anxiety, peer use,

FIGURE 1.1

Summary of Theoretical Framework

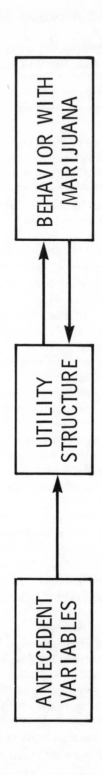

or parental permissiveness. That link is not included in Figure 1.1 because it is not tested in this study.

HYPOTHESES

It is now possible to state more explicitly the basic hypotheses that evolved from this framework and guided this research. With each hypothesis there is indicated in parentheses the chapter in which the hypothesis is addressed by the data. Each hypothesis pertains predominantly to persons who were 12 and 13 years of age at the beginning of the study.

1. Among those who have never used marijuana, the more positive the utility structure, the more likely it is that marijuana will be used within one year (Chapter 5).
2. Among those who have used marijuana, the more positive the utility structure, the more likely it is that marijuana has been used recently (Chapter 6).
3. Among those who have used marijuana, the more positive the utility structure, the more likely it is that marijuana has been used frequently (Chapter 6).
4. The utility structure is a stronger correlate of marijuana behavior than other variables considered to be determinants of marijuana behavior (Chapter 7).
5. The utility structure explains why selected antecedent variables and marijuana behavior are related (Chapter 8).
6. The utility structure changes more during a year for those who become users of marijuana than for those who remain nonusers (Chapter 9).
7. Among those who have used marijuana, the utility structure of those who used it recently changes more than for those who have not used it recently (Chapter 9).
8. Among those who have used marijuana, the utility structure of those who used it frequently changes more than for those who did not use it frequently (Chapter 9).

Two additional hypotheses guided the analyses. First, when considering the utility structure conceptually it was assumed that all components of the utility structure—attribute, salience, subjective probability, delayed consequence, time orientation—were necessary for an adequate explanation of behavior with marijuana. This assumption is tested empirically through the following hypothesis:

9. Each of the components of the utility structure adds to the explanation of behavior with marijuana (Chapters 5 and 6).

Second, as described in detail in Chapter 2, through literature review and pilot studies many attributes included in the measure of the utility structure were identified. Beginning with all these attributes is not tantamount to concluding that each attribute is necessary for explaining behavior. If fewer attributes than were originally identified are adequate for explaining behavior then, as discussed in Chapter 10, a reduction in the number of attributes could refine the theory, lead to improved measurement of the utility structure, and also have practical significance. Thus, the following hypothesis is also tested.

10. A reduced set of attributes explains behavior with marijuana as well as the full set of attributes selected initially for study (Chapter 10).

RELATED LITERATURE

The statement on utility theory here considered classic is Jeremy Bentham's treatise of 1780. He postulated that all behavior is derived from weighing its good and bad consequences. Bentham included most of the components of utility structure used in this study. More recent considerations of many different utility models have been summarized for the fields of economics (Page 1957) and psychology (Edwards 1954; Lee 1971; Rapoport and Wallsten, 1972; Slovic, Fischoff, and Lichtenstein 1977).

The notion that people behave in accordance with the ratio of positive to negative consequences is basic to many theories of human behavior, including learning, social action, social exchange, socialization, and achievement motivation. Simon (1957) used it to explain behavior that ranged from playing chess to the dynamics of corporations. It has been used to explain why people do not use health services (Rosenstock 1966; Udry and Morris 1971) and to account for compliance with the regimen recommended by such services (Becker and Maiman 1975). The principle has been applied to explain such supposedly diverse activities as choosing an occupation (Huber, Daneshgar, and Ford 1971; Mitchell and Beach 1975), deciding whether to have a baby (Jaccard and Davidson 1976; Werner, Middlestadt-Carter, and Crawford 1975), and drinking alcohol (Schlegel, Crawford, and Sandborn 1977).

There appears to have been no previous research that has tested hypotheses that incorporate the utility structure and the drug behavior of young people. Thus, it is paradoxical that most considerations of drug behavior include some reference to the consequences associated with that behavior. The list of consequences in Table 1.1 was compiled from research on drug behavior—research that is important to this study because it supports the basic assumption that the consequences of drugs are central to drug behavior, and serves as one of the sources for identifying a comprehensive set of attributes. However, no research has considered that anticipated consequences might be important to subsequent behavior and subjected this to systematic tests within the context of the version of utility theory set forth here.

The concept of attributes is approached by research that asks people why they do or do not use various drugs; several such studies are cited here. Bowden (1971) used information from five clinical cases to suggest that people begin using opiates because they perceive such benefits as pleasure, satisfaction of curiosity, and increased control over aggression and anger. Halikas, Goodwin, and Guze (1971) asked 100 marijuana users to complete a checklist of 105 effects of marijuana. Brown et al. (1971) asked heroin users why they began and terminated the use of heroin, and all the reasons can be classified as positive and negative consequences. Eells (1968) asked college students about the beneficial and harmful nature of drugs and why they used drugs, and found such positive outcomes as satisfaction of curiosity, kicks, self-evaluation, escape from problems, and reduction of boredom. Costs of drugs included medical risks and the possibility of legal problems. Blumenfield et al. (1972) studied marijuana use among senior high school students, and identified such consequences as pleasure, tension reduction, understanding of self and others, a feeling of closeness to God, creativity, and happiness. Rouse and Ewing (1973) found similar positive consequences associated with drug use among college students. These should suffice as examples of research that ask for the rationale underlying behavior and about the consequences of drugs. However, these studies did not measure the anticipated consequences among users and nonusers of drugs and relate them to subsequent drug behavior in the manner suggested by the theory presented here.

Separate treatment is given to Kalant and Kalant (1971) because their approach to considering drug behavior represents an explicit recognition of the portion of utility theory that acknowledges the importance of the imbalance of anticipated consequences. Kalant and Kalant reviewed research on drug use and concluded that, in the final analysis, each individual must weigh the benefits that would be experienced through drug use against the costs. They summarized that aspect of utility when they proposed that there are

> relative weights we attach to different "beneficial" and "harmful" consequences of drug use and of legislative control of drug use. These are things which every

citizen has to balance for himself, because probably
no two citizens share exactly the same scale of relative values. To work with these, we must pose a
variety of balance-seeking questions. For instance,
how much pleasure and individual freedom with respect to drug use is worth how much physical,
psychiatric, or social damage to the victims of excessive drug use? (Kalant and Kalant 1971, p. 123)

Kalant and Kalant did not test this reasoning directly, and did not
consider the potential importance of such components as time orientation and subjective probability. Moreover, they were primarily
concerned with utility as it relates to making decisions for society,
whereas the concern here is primarily with the decisions individuals
make regarding their own behavior. However, they did consider the
imbalance of anticipated consequence basic to decisions about drug
use and in a more explicit fashion than most treatments.

Blum et al. (1970) considered the ratio of positive and negative consequences empirically—an element necessary to the utility
variable—but devoted less than a page of their 400-page book to that
ratio. Using retrospective reports of what good and bad effects accrued from marijuana and hallucinogens, they noted that the ratio
of positive to negative reports was much greater for students who
had used hallucinogens than for those who had used marijuana. Although their research suggests promise for utility theory, it is not
a substitute for this present research for several reasons. Not all
positive and negative effects were identified; it did not incorporate
the person who has never used drugs, nor did it consider frequency
of drug use and continuation; it was retrospective, for one does not
know whether drug behavior produced the effects or the effects the
behavior; Blum was concerned with actual consequences, not with
anticipated consequences; and most components of the utility structure were not included.

Studies published since this research began contain ingredients
that approximate the theory more closely than earlier studies.
Weinstein (1977) reported significant relationships between marijuana use and expectations regarding the interpersonal consequences
of using marijuana. Two studies used criminal deterrence theory
as a guide (Silberman 1976; Meier and Johnson 1977) and found that
the perceived threat of legal punishment is related to use of marijuana. Pomazal and Brown (1977) found that specific beliefs con-
cerning marijuana effects differentiated those who had used marijuana from those who had not, and that those beliefs about effects
were strongly related to intentions to use marijuana in the future.
Albrecht and Carpenter (1976) examined two theories about attitude-

behavior relationships, and found that attitudes toward marijuana
and perceptions about how others would view use of marijuana were
related to use of marijuana. These studies suggest promise for the
application of utility theory to explain behavior with marijuana.
However, none can be considered substitutes for the research reported here. First, all these studies used cross-sectional rather
than panel designs, and therefore the possibility of reciprocal relationships between anticipated consequences and behavior cannot be
examined empirically. Second, those studies had college students
as participants, and the subjects in this study were of an age when
relatively few have used marijuana. Third, none of the studies considers all the components of utility structure embodied in the model
presented here. Finally, three of the studies (Weinstein, Silberman,
Meier and Johnson) restrict the domain of anticipated consequences—
for example, to interpersonal or legal consequences—whereas the
formulation in this study suggests that a broader range of consequences should be considered. In this latter respect this research
is more similar to the studies by Pomazal and Brown, and by
Albrecht and Carpenter.

Many studies have attempted to identify the social and psychological correlates of drug behavior. These variables comprise the
antecedent variables listed in Table 1.2. The reviews by Jessor
(1979), Kandel (1978), and Lettieri (1975) do such a good job of
summarizing and citing the relevant studies that it has seemed unnecessary to cite all the relevant literature in this book. Most of
the studies that relate antecedent variables to marijuana demonstrated weak relationships. That might be in part due to the lack of
an adequate theoretical model to guide research. Much of the earlier
research does not measure the variables that might provide the link
between drug behavior and the social and psychological variables,
and measuring the linkage variables could substantially increase the
amount of variance explained. In this research the utility structure
is considered an important link. Few research efforts that have
identified social and psychological correlates of drug behavior explicitly use the utility notion to interpret correlations.

SIGNIFICANCE

Considerable research has been done in an attempt to identify
the determinants of marijuana use, but these studies leave much of
the variation in that behavior unexplained. The present study was
begun with the belief that the theory has an unusually good chance of
explaining marijuana use because it has a firm foundation in many
other theories of human behavior, and because some of the components

of the utility structure are found in most considerations of drug behavior. Thus, confirmation of hypotheses that stem from the theory could improve the understanding of marijuana behavior.

This version of the utility model was considered to have particular appeal because it provides organization to the infinite number of variables considered to cause marijuana behavior. When viewing much of the earlier research on marijuana behavior as a whole, one is impressed by the sheer number of different variables offered as determinants of behavior, and the lack of schemes for grouping such variables in meaningful ways. When ten people are asked why adolescents do or do not smoke marijuana, many more than ten explanations are received, and the possible interrelationships among the variables imbedded in the explanations are typically far from clear. When viewing all the attributes listed in Table 1.1 and the antecedent variables shown in Table 1.2, and taking each as a separate variable that might contribute to an understanding of marijuana behavior, one is faced with such a conglomerate of variables that using them to understand behavior can become an exercise in futility. Thus, it was felt that some organization was required for variables such as these, and that this order might be accomplished by the theory outlined here. The many attributes are combined in one variable: the utility structure. Moreover, included within that variable are other explanations for marijuana behavior, such as subjective probability and time orientation. Furthermore, this variable is placed in a causal chain of reasoning with other variables grouped together as antecedent. The model chosen to guide this research provides an organization for variables, and this organization could contribute to understanding behavior.

What would be the value of this research if the hypotheses derived from the theory were confirmed by rigorous test? There are multiple answers to that question. First, understanding why people behave as they do regarding marijuana might contribute to explaining other human behavior. In general, that might apply to any behavior involving choice. In particular, although consideration here has been restricted to marijuana, it would suggest that behavior with other drugs might be better understood if the theory explains use of marijuana. The hypothesis in this case would be that different drugs have different utility structures, but other than that, the theory would read essentially the same if applied to such diverse drugs as heroin, LSD, or alcohol. Second, the theory proposes to explain why the antecedent variables are related to marijuana use. If the utility structure is an important link, the earlier research could be more readily understood and future research more properly designed. Third, the utility structure, when compared with many other variables considered to be causes of marijuana use, could be responsive to intervention. This is not the case for such variables as race, sex, and place of residence. Thus, it is believed that this research could make a meaningful contribution to policy and programs. Finally, it is believed that Lee (1971) is correct in concluding that one reason there is not more research guided by utility theory in the field setting is the complexity of measurement required. Verification of hypotheses from the theory using data collected from young people would suggest that measures can be obtained on adolescents in the field setting. The significance of this research is considered again in the final chapter of this book where the implications of the findings are discussed.

THE USE OF UTILITY THEORY

The forms that utility theory can take vary substantially within and across disciplines. This research fits none of the forms perfectly, and it fits some very imperfectly. Given a research design that required data from a large number of subjects and a limitation of time to collect a substantial amount of information from each subject, the fact that the mathematical assumptions and rigor of measurement required by some utility theorists were not approached is a matter of some concern. Consideration was given to not using the term utility theory in this book to avoid this discrepancy. In the final analysis utility theory was chosen over other words to describe the theoretical orientation because the central premise of utility theory—that the positive and negative consequences of behavior are of fundamental relevance to behavior—is basic to this research, because the conduct of the research was influenced more by the various considerations of utility theory than any other theoretical orientation, and because it is hoped that this may stimulate future research that will be able to conform more perfectly to the various canons demanded by the more advanced formulations of utility theory. Meanwhile, it is acknowledged that a version of a theory of utility is being considered, rather than any single theory that has been advanced by others. Readers who prefer to think of this research as more akin to such frameworks as those provided by a subjective, expected utility model or an expectancy-value theory of attitudes (Fishbein and Ajzen 1975) are welcome to do so. However, they will note that in some respects here also there has been a departure from these approaches.

REFERENCES

Albrecht, Stan L., and Kerry E. Carpenter. "Attitudes as Predictors of Behavior versus Behavior Intentions: A Convergence of Research Traditions." Sociometry 39 (1976): 1-10.

Becker, Marshall H., and Lois A. Maiman. "Sociobehavioral Determinants of Compliance with Health and Medical Recommendations." Medical Care 13 (1975): 10-24.

Bentham, Jeremy. A Fragment on Government and An Introduction to the Principles of Morals and Legislation. Edited by Wilfred Harrison. Oxford: Basil Blackwell, 1948. (Originally printed in 1780.)

Blum, Richard H., and Associates. Drugs II: Students and Drugs— College and High School Observations. San Francisco: Jossey-Bass, 1970.

Blumenfield, Michael, et al. "Marijuana Use in High School Students." Diseases of the Nervous System 33 (1972): 603-10.

Bowden, Charles L. "Determinants of Initial Use of Opioids." Comprehensive Psychiatry 12 (1971): 136-40.

Brown, Barry S., et al. "In Their Own Words: Addicts' Reasons for Initiating and Withdrawing from Heroin." International Journal of the Addictions 6 (1971): 638.

Edwards, Ward. "The Theory of Decision Making." Psychological Bulletin 51 (1954): 380-417.

Eells, Kenneth. "Marijuana and LSD—A Survey of One College Campus." Journal of Counseling Psychology 15 (1968): 459-67.

Fishbein, Martin, and Icek Ajzen. Belief, Attitude, Intention and Behavior: An Introduction to Theory and Research. Reading, Mass.: Addison-Wesley, 1975.

Halikas, James A., Donald W. Goodwin, and Samuel B. Guze. "Marihuana Effects—A Survey of Regular Users." Journal of the American Medical Association 217 (1971): 692-94.

Huber, George P., Rahman Daneshgar, and David L. Ford. "An Empirical Comparison of Five Utility Models for Predicting Job Preference." Organizational Behavior and Human Performance 6 (1971): 267-82.

Jaccard, James J., and Andrew R. Davidson. "The Relation of Psychological, Social, and Economic Variables to Fertility-Related Decisions." Demography 13 (1976): 329-38.

Jessor, Richard. "Marijuana: A Review of Recent Psychosocial Research." In Handbook on Drug Abuse, edited by Robert I. Dupont, Avram Goldstein, and John O'Donnel, pp. 337-55. Washington, D.C.: Government Printing Office, 1979.

Kalant, Harold, and Oriana Josseau Kalant. Drugs, Society and Personal Choice. Ontario: Paperjacks and the Addiction Research Foundation of Toronto, 1972.

Kandel, Denise, ed. Longitudinal Research on Drug Use: Empirical Findings and Methodological Issues. New York: Wiley, 1978.

Lee, Wayne. Decision Theory and Human Behavior. New York: Wiley, 1971.

Lettieri, Dan J., ed. Predicting Adolescent Drug Abuse: A Review of Issues, Methods and Correlates. Washington, D.C.: Government Printing Office, 1975.

Meier, Robert F., and Weldon T. Johnson. "Deterrence as Social Control: The Legal and Extralegal Production of Conformity." American Sociological Review 42 (1977): 292-304.

Mitchell, Terence R., and Lee Roy Beach. Expectancy Theory, Decision Theory and Occupational Preference and Choice. Seattle: University of Washington, 1975.

Page, Alfred N. Utility Theory: A Book of Readings. New York: Wiley, 1957.

Pomazal, Richard J., and James D. Brown. "Understanding Drug Use Motivation: A New Look at a Current Problem." Journal of Health and Social Behavior 18 (1977): 212-22.

Rapoport, Amnon, and Thomas S. Wallsten. "Individual Decision Behavior." Annual Review of Psychology 23 (1972): 131-76.

Rosenstock, Irwin W. "Why People Use Health Services." Milbank Memorial Fund Quarterly 44 (1966): 94-124.

Rouse, Beatrice A., and John A. Ewing. "Marijuana and Other Drug Use by Women College Students: Associated Risk Taking and Coping Activities." American Journal of Psychiatry 130 (1973): 486-91.

Schlegal, Ronald P., Craig A. Crawford, and Margaret D. Sandborn. "Correspondence and Mediational Properties of the Fishbein Model: An Application to Adolescent Alcohol Use." Journal of Experimental Social Psychology 13 (1977): 421-30.

Silberman, Matthew. "Toward a Theory of Criminal Deterrence." American Sociological Review 41 (1976): 442-61.

Simon, Herbert A. Models of Man: Social and Rational. New York: Wiley, 1957.

Slovic, Paul, Baruch Fischoff, and Sarah Lichtenstein. "Behavioral Decision Theory." Annual Review of Psychology 28 (1977): 1-39.

Udry, J. Richard, and Naomi M. Morris. "A Spoonful of Sugar Helps the Medicine Go Down." American Journal of Public Health 61 (1971): 776-85.

Weinstein, Raymond M. "The Imputation of Motives for Marijuana Behavior." The International Journal of the Addictions 11 (1976): 571-95.

Werner, Paul D., Susan E. Middlestadt-Carter, and Thomas J. Crawford. "Having a Third Child: Predicting Behavioral Intentions." Journal of Marriage and the Family 37 (1975): 348-58.

2
RESEARCH DESIGN AND QUESTIONNAIRE

This chapter first discusses why a panel design was considered to be prerequisite for an adequate test of the hypotheses. The rationale for choosing seventh graders to enter the panel is then presented. This leads to a description of the school system that served as the research locale. There is a brief digression to indicate how the research strategy represents a modification of what was originally planned. Finally, the questionnaire is presented.

THE PANEL DESIGN

A cross-sectional design, in which data would have been gathered only once, was considered unacceptable for testing the hypotheses. Acceptable tests of all the hypotheses required the use of a panel design; that is, data had to be collected from the same individuals more than once. Although both cross-sectional and panel designs would allow a determination as to whether an association existed between the utility structure and behavior—which is one type of evidence necessary for inferring a causal connection between these variables—only a panel design would provide information necessary to determine whether the utility structure influenced behavior, or behavior influenced the utility structure, or whether there was a reciprocal relationship between these variables. A panel design, for example, allows measuring the utility structure at one point in time for those who have never used marijuana, and then predicting their later behavior with marijuana. This was considered prequisite to making a reasonable inference about the influence of the utility structure on behavior. If a cross-sectional design were used, and showed a relationship between the utility structure and behavior, it would not be possible to determine whether marijuana use varied before or after the utility structure, and therefore from that association it could not be inferred with confidence that the utility structure influenced behavior; an equally plausible conclusion from the cross-sectional design would be that behavior influenced the utility structure. Given the hypothesized reciprocal relationship between the utility structure and behavior, a panel rather than a cross-sectional design was used to provide evidence about the time relationship between variables.

SEVENTH GRADERS AS PARTICIPANTS

The measurements were begun when subjects were in the seventh grade, for five reasons. First, data from Charlotte-Mecklenburg, North Carolina, collected in the spring of 1972 (McLeod and Grizzle 1972) showed a substantial increase in drug use between grades seven and nine, with a lower rate of increase in drug use in the tenth grade and beyond. Their data are shown in Figure 2.1, and are similar to the findings of other studies conducted several years earlier (Glenn and Richards 1974). These trends suggest that many youths make decisions about drug use after the seventh grade, which makes this an ideal time to assess the value of the hypotheses derived from utility theory. Second, from a methodological standpoint, the rate of increase between seventh and eighth grades provides acceptable distributions of respondents according to the dependent variable "ever used marijuana" from the perspectives of sampling and analysis—perhaps an optimal distribution compared with any other period. Third, it was thought that working with the administrative structures of junior high schools, rather than those of both elementary and senior high schools, should simplify data gathering somewhat, and it is presumed that the quality of data will be reflected by this simplicity. Fourth, it was assumed that obtaining a grant for this research that would extend beyond three years was very unlikely. Because of a constraint on time for data gathering, and for reasons given earlier in this paragraph, beginning with seventh graders is as good as, or better than, using other grades that also would have permitted the completion of the study within three years. Finally, when the research was begun there was an impression that school systems would be more willing to introduce educational programs about drugs at the junior high level than at lower grades. Thus, it was felt that the findings from junior high school subjects could be applicable to the design of programs for schools.

FIGURE 2.1

Percentage of Students by Grade Who Have Used
Marijuana in Charlotte-Mecklenburg Junior
and Senior High Schools, March 1972

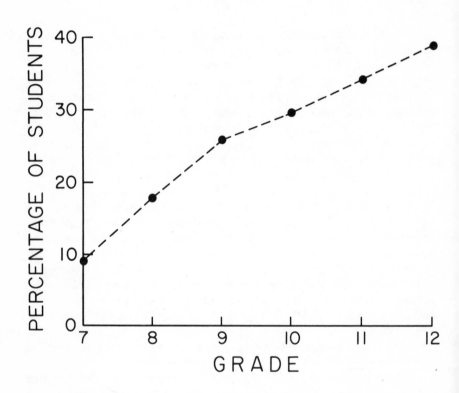

Source: Jonnie H. McLeod and Gloria A. Grizzle, Alcohol and
Other Drug Usage among Junior and Senior High School Students in
Charlotte-Mecklenburg (Chapel Hill, N.C.: Institute of Government,
1974). Adapted with permission of the Charlotte Drug Education Cen-
ter, Inc., and the Institute of Government of the University of North
Carolina at Chapel Hill.

THE RESEARCH LOCALE

The criteria used to select the research locale were that the
schools have no attribute that might preclude adequate test of the
hypotheses, that the school system have between 2,000 and 3,000
seventh graders, that the seventh graders exhibit considerable het-
erogeneity with respect to social and demographic characteristics,
that there be few rather than many schools for the sake of enhancing
data quality and minimizing the budget, that the schools be located
in areas not too atypical when compared with other areas, and that
the research be located close enough to the research office in Chapel
Hill so that data-gathering activities would not be hampered in any
way by distance, and so that the budget could be minimized. Since
private schools attract only 2.4 percent of the elementary students
in North Carolina (U.S. Bureau of the Census, 1972), the study was
restricted to students in public schools. With those criteria in mind
the search began for an appropriate school system in North Carolina
to serve as the research locale.

The Chapel Hill-Carrboro city schools and the Orange County
schools, located in the same town and county as the research base
at the University of North Carolina at Chapel Hill, were never considered seriously as the research locale: their combined seventh
grade population was only 915. However, the Chapel Hill-Carrboro
city schools did contribute to the research by collaborating on the
initial pilot studies discussed later in this chapter.

The next locales considered were the two public school systems in Wake County, North Carolina: the Wake County schools,
and the Raleigh public schools. Together they had 4,608 seventh
graders (2,763 in the Wake County schools and 1,845 in the Raleigh
public schools). The administrative offices for both were located
within several blocks of each other in Raleigh, and the research
staff in Chapel Hill could reach those offices by car in less than 40
minutes. The students in those systems exhibit considerable het-
erogeneity with respect to selected social and demographic characteristics, and the areas in which they are located are not atypical.
There appeared to be nothing about the Wake County schools that
would be unfavorable for testing the hypotheses. The Wake County
schools agreed to collaborate, and the students in the eight largest
schools were chosen for participation because these schools had a
sufficient number of students. The ninth largest school in the system served as a locale for pilot studies, and no data were collected
in the two smallest schools.

Wake County contained 228,453 inhabitants at the time of the
study. Raleigh, the capital city of North Carolina, is located in
Wake County, and with a population of 121,031 is the fourth largest

city in the state. However, persons living in Raleigh attended the
Raleigh public schools rather than the schools used in this study.
The vast majority of students in the Wake County schools lived in
urban areas. Table 2.1 shows the median years of school completed by persons 25 years of age and older, the median family in-
come, and the percent of families below poverty level for Raleigh,
for Wake County, for North Carolina, and for the United States.
These data provide a rough gauge of how comparable the areas are
with respect to those socioeconomic variables. Each variable indicated that, on the average, Raleigh had higher socioeconomic status
than North Carolina, and North Carolina had lower socioeconomic
status than the total U.S. population. Wake County was similar to
the United States as a whole on these three indicators.

TABLE 2.1

Selected Social and Economic Characteristics of Raleigh,
Wake County, North Carolina, and the United States

Area	Median Years of School Completed by Persons 25 Years of Age and Older	Median Annual Family Income	Percent of Families below Poverty Level
Raleigh	12.4	$10,085	10.3
Wake County	12.2	9,557	11.2
North Carolina	10.6	7,774	16.3
United States	12.1	9,590	10.7

Sources: U.S. Bureau of the Census, Census of the Population: 1970: General Social and Economic Characteristics, Final
Report PC(1)-C-35, North Carolina (Washington, D.C.: U.S. Government Printing Office, 1972), Tables 40, 43, and 44; U.S. Bureau
of the Census, Census of the Population: 1970: General Social and
Economic Characteristics, Final Report PC(1)-C1, United States
Summary (Washington, D.C.: U.S. Government Printing Office,
1972), Tables 75, 83, and 95.

There is no intention to leave the impression that what is described above conforms exactly with what was originally planned.
As is true for any research project with a degree of complexity, it
was necessary to deviate from the initial plans. More ambitious

research was originally proposed to the granting agency, which would have included more drugs than marijuana for study, a sample four times the size obtained, and collection of data from the subjects three times rather than twice. What was planned would have required much more time to complete, and much greater expenditures than the agency was willing to provide. The granting agency believed that the project should be more modest since there was no comparable research on the utility structure as it pertained to drugs. They were particularly concerned about the lack of precedence for measuring the utility structure as it relates to drug behavior, and the researchers considered that to be their most difficult task.

INTRODUCTION TO THE QUESTIONNAIRE

Measurement of the utility structure was considered to be a major challenge of the research: there had been few prior studies conducted in a field situation to provide guidance, and the measures would have to be readily comprehended by seventh graders. To minimize budget it was decided to use self-administered questionnaires rather than interviews, and this required rigorous attention to the development of the questionnaires and procedures for administering them. The most immediate concern was how to obtain information on the utility structure by using questionnaires that would yield valid tests of the hypotheses. Specific questions about collecting data to measure this critical variable were the following:

1. Should an open-ended approach be used—in which subjects would be relied upon to generate anticipated consequences of marijuana without any being suggested—or would it be better to present all subjects with the same list of anticipated consequences?
2. Researchers' time with subjects would be limited to about 90 minutes. If lists of consequences were provided to subjects, which should be included to represent sufficient coverage of the universe of consequences?
3. What words, instructions, and procedures would be readily understood by nearly all of the young subjects?
4. What measures of salience and subjective probability would be understood by most seventh graders?

These questions were first addressed by discussing them with a wide range of experts, such as school administrators, teachers, utility theorists, and researchers. Junior high school students were also included in the discussions. Also, the lists of consequences presented in Table 1.1 and the literature from which they were gleaned were reexamined. None of these activities produced final answers to the questions, but their contribution provided the basis for proceeding with the pilot studies implemented to develop measures of the utility structure.

PILOT STUDIES

The first pilot study was conducted with ten seventh graders at one of the two junior high schools in the Chapel Hill-Carrboro (North Carolina) city schools. The subjects were administered a questionnaire designed to collect information essential for measuring the utility structure. The questionnaires were administered in a one-to-one situation, and there were detailed discussions with each subject during and after completion of the questionnaire. From this experience it was possible to identify words and instructions that were not understood, add attributes to the lists, and elicit many suggestions for improving the questionnaires. Also, it was determined that an open-ended format was unfeasible, and that the closed approach appeared to be workable. On the basis of this experience a new questionnaire was developed.

The new questionnaire was administered to 24 seventh graders in the second junior high school of the Chapel Hill-Carrboro city schools. This pilot study had the same objectives as the first. In addition, it made it possible to test the questionnaire in a group-administered rather than a one-to-one situation, and there were enough subjects to enable the researchers to determine whether or not they were obtaining adequate variation in the variables. Open-ended questions were included to identify more attributes that should be added. Also, the subjects were debriefed in order to identify sources of confusion and words that were misunderstood. The questionnaire and the data collection procedures were then refined for a third pilot study.

The next pilot study was with 146 seventh graders at the junior high school in Knightdale, North Carolina. This was the first attempt to administer the questionnaire to a large group. After administering the questionnaire to all 146 subjects at one time, it was evident that smaller groups were more manageable and would provide data of higher quality. Since this school was in the same system as the schools in the larger study, this pilot also made it possible to determine that there was sufficient use of marijuana in the system to provide adequate data for the study, and that students in this school system could understand the questionnaire and procedures as well as those in the other pilot schools. Prior

to this pilot study there had been some limited piloting of the items
to be used to measure variables other than those related to the utility structure, because there was considerable prior research available for guidance. Thus, these measures were also tested with this
pilot sample. Finally, there were enough subjects in this pilot to
conduct correlation analyses to determine whether the measures of
the utility structure were associated with other variables such as
past use of marijuana. These analyses did produce strong correlations in the hypothesized directions. It was concluded that minor
refinements in the questionnaire were to be made on the basis of the
experience in Knightdale and that further pilots were unnecessary.

THE QUESTIONNAIRE

The questionnaire that resulted from this seven-month process
(June through December 1975) has three sections: Section A includes
measures of the positive attributes and the salience and subjective
probability of each, Section B includes these measures for the negative consequences, and Section C includes items to measure all
other variables. The entire questionnaire is in Appendix A.

Section A of the questionnaire is reproduced in Table 2.2.
The consequences were listed randomly. Subjects were instructed
to mark the positive consequences they thought might occur as a result of marijuana use and to leave unmarked those consequences
they thought would not occur (see first page of Table 2.2). Their
marks went through to the next two pages so that subjects could
judge salience and subjective probability for only those consequences
they anticipated. This procedure was used to reduce fatigue, time
for completing the questionnaire, and confusion that occurred during
the initial pilot studies when subjects were asked to judge salience
and subjective probability for consequences they did not anticipate.
Subjects then marked the second part of Section A to indicate salience and then completed the third part to assess subjective probability. They then completed Section B for the negative consequences and Section C which contained the items for all other
variables in the study (Appendix A).

Before beginning the questionnaire, subjects were given instructions for completing Sections A and B of the questionnaire by
using a non-drug-related example of the consequences of not carrying an umbrella. This was presented verbally to the subjects,
using an enlarged version of the visual aid shown in Appendix B,
with as much time as necessary allowed for clarifying any aspects
of this process.

TABLE 2.2

First Three Pages of Questionnaire

From the list below, pick out the GOOD THINGS that you think might happen to you if you used marijuana (grass, pot, reefers). Check each THING you pick out.

___ GET HIGH (GET THRILLS OR KICKS, HAVE A GOOD TIME)
___ HAVE OTHER KIDS THINK THAT I AM COOL
___ FEEL AS IF TIME WERE PASSING SLOWER
___ HAVE MORE SELF-CONFIDENCE
___ BE ABLE TO DO THINGS BETTER
___ FEEL MORE PLEASURE (FEEL GOOD)
___ FEEL CLOSER TO OTHERS
___ ENJOY DOING THINGS WITH MY FRIENDS
___ FEEL STRONGER
___ ENJOY THE TASTE
___ UNDERSTAND MYSELF BETTER
___ ACT AGAINST MY PARENTS, OTHER ADULTS OR SOCIETY (TO REBEL)
___ FEEL AT HOME WITH THE GROUP
___ SEE, SMELL, TASTE, HEAR OR FEEL THINGS BETTER
___ BE LESS BORED
___ HAVE LESS PAIN
___ WORRY LESS (BE ABLE TO FORGET ABOUT PROBLEMS FOR A WHILE)
___ HAVE DIFFERENT OR INTERESTING THOUGHTS
___ FEEL MORE IMPORTANT OR GROWN-UP
___ SLEEP BETTER
___ FEEL HAPPIER (NOT FEEL SO "LOW," OR DOWN IN THE DUMPS OR DEPRESSED)
___ BE ABLE TO THINK BETTER (FOR EXAMPLE, REMEMBER THINGS BETTER, LEARN FASTER, HAVE BETTER CONCENTRATION, SOLVE MY PROBLEMS BETTER, GET BETTER GRADES)
___ BE MORE RELAXED
___ HELP ME CONTROL MY WEIGHT
___ SATISFY MY CURIOSITY (FIND OUT WHAT IT IS LIKE)
___ BE LIKED MORE BY MY FRIENDS OR HAVE MORE FRIENDS

ONLY for the THINGS YOU MARKED, answer the questions by
writing one of the following numbers beside your mark.
1   UNIMPORTANT   2   ONLY SLIGHTLY IMPORTANT
3   SOMEWHAT IMPORTANT   4   QUITE IMPORTANT
5   VERY VERY IMPORTANT

___ How important is it to you to GET HIGH (GET THRILLS OR
     KICKS, HAVE A GOOD TIME)?
___ How important is it to you for OTHER KIDS TO THINK THAT
     YOU ARE COOL?
___ How important is it to you to FEEL AS IF TIME WERE
     PASSING SLOWER?
___ How important is it to you to HAVE MORE SELF-CONFIDENCE?
___ How important is it to you to BE ABLE TO DO THINGS BETTER?
___ How important is it to you to FEEL MORE PLEASURE (FEEL
     GOOD)?
___ How important is it to you to FEEL CLOSER TO OTHERS?
___ How important is it to you to ENJOY DOING THINGS WITH
     YOUR FRIENDS?
___ How important is it to you to FEEL STRONGER?
___ How important is it to you to ENJOY THE TASTE OF SOME-
     THING?
___ How important is it to you to UNDERSTAND YOURSELF BETTER?
___ How important is it to you to ACT AGAINST YOUR PARENTS,
     OTHER ADULTS, OR SOCIETY (TO REBEL)?
___ How important is it to you to FEEL AT HOME WITH THE GROUP?
___ How important is it to you to SEE, SMELL, TASTE, HEAR OR
     FEEL THINGS BETTER?
___ How important is it to you to BE LESS BORED?
___ How important is it to you to HAVE LESS PAIN?
___ How important is it to you to WORRY LESS (BE ABLE TO
     FORGET ABOUT PROBLEMS FOR A WHILE)?
___ How important is it to you to HAVE DIFFERENT OR INTEREST-
     ING THOUGHTS?
___ How important is it to you to FEEL MORE IMPORTANT AND
     GROWN-UP?
___ How important is it to you to SLEEP BETTER?
___ How important is it to you to FEEL HAPPIER (NOT FEEL SO
     "LOW" OR DOWN IN THE DUMPS OR DEPRESSED)?
___ How important is it to you to BE ABLE TO THINK BETTER
     (FOR EXAMPLE, REMEMBER THINGS BETTER, LEARN
     FASTER, HAVE BETTER CONCENTRATION, SOLVE YOUR
     PROBLEMS BETTER, GET BETTER GRADES)?

(continued)

Table 2.2 continued

___ How important is it to you to BE MORE RELAXED?
___ How important is it to you to CONTROL YOUR WEIGHT?
___ How important is it to you to SATISFY YOUR CURIOSITY
(FIND OUT WHAT NEW THINGS ARE LIKE)?
___ How important is it to you to BE LIKED MORE BY YOUR
FRIENDS OR HAVE MORE FRIENDS?

ONLY for the THINGS YOU MARKED, answer the questions by
writing one of the following numbers beside your mark.
1 IMPOSSIBLE   2 NOT VERY LIKELY   3 SOMEWHAT LIKELY
4 VERY LIKELY   5 ABSOLUTELY CERTAIN

___ If you used marijuana, how LIKELY is it that you would GET
HIGH (GET THRILLS OR KICKS, HAVE A GOOD TIME)?
___ If you used marijuana, how LIKELY is it that OTHER KIDS
WOULD THINK THAT YOU WERE COOL?
___ If you used marijuana, how LIKELY is it that you would FEEL
AS IF TIME WERE PASSING SLOWER?
___ If you used marijuana, how LIKELY is it that you would HAVE
MORE SELF-CONFIDENCE?
___ If you used marijuana, how LIKELY is it that you would BE
ABLE TO DO THINGS BETTER?
___ If you used marijuana, how LIKELY is it that you would FEEL
MORE PLEASURE (FEEL GOOD)?
___ If you used marijuana, how LIKELY is it that you would FEEL
CLOSER TO OTHERS?
___ If you used marijuana, how LIKELY is it that you would ENJOY
DOING THINGS WITH YOUR FRIENDS?
___ If you used marijuana, how LIKELY is it that you would FEEL
STRONGER?
___ If you used marijuana, how LIKELY is it that you would ENJOY
THE TASTE?
___ If you used marijuana, how LIKELY is it that you would
UNDERSTAND YOURSELF BETTER?
___ If you used marijuana, how LIKELY is it that you would ACT
AGAINST YOUR PARENTS, OTHER ADULTS, OR SOCIETY
(TO REBEL)?

____ If you used marijuana, how LIKELY is it that you would FEEL AT HOME WITH THE GROUP?

____ If you used marijuana, how LIKELY is it that you would SEE, SMELL, TASTE, HEAR OR FEEL THINGS BETTER?

____ If you used marijuana, how LIKELY is it that you would BE LESS BORED?

____ If you used marijuana, how LIKELY is it that you would HAVE LESS PAIN?

____ If you used marijuana, how LIKELY is it that you would WORRY LESS (BE ABLE TO FORGET ABOUT PROBLEMS FOR A WHILE)?

____ If you used marijuana, how LIKELY is it that you would HAVE DIFFERENT OR INTERESTING THOUGHTS?

____ If you used marijuana, how LIKELY is it that you would FEEL MORE IMPORTANT OR GROWN-UP?

____ If you used marijuana, how LIKELY is it that you would SLEEP BETTER?

____ If you used marijuana, how LIKELY is it that you would FEEL HAPPIER (NOT FEEL SO "LOW," OR DOWN IN THE DUMPS OR DEPRESSED)?

____ If you used marijuana, how LIKELY is it that you would BE ABLE TO THINK BETTER (FOR EXAMPLE, REMEMBER THINGS BETTER, LEARN FASTER, HAVE BETTER CONCENTRATION, SOLVE YOUR PROBLEMS BETTER, GET BETTER GRADES)?

____ If you used marijuana, how LIKELY is it that you would BE MORE RELAXED?

____ If you used marijuana, how LIKELY is it that it would HELP YOU CONTROL YOUR WEIGHT?

____ If you used marijuana, how LIKELY is it that it would SATISFY YOUR CURIOSITY (FIND OUT WHAT IT IS LIKE)?

____ If you used marijuana, how LIKELY is it that you would BE LIKED MORE BY YOUR FRIENDS OR HAVE MORE FRIENDS?

Most of the items in Section C of the questionnaire were from questions found related to drug behavior in earlier studies (see, for example, Nehemkis, Macari, and Lettieri 1976) and adapted for this research during the pilot studies. The antecedent variables were chosen on the basis of their consistent relationships with marijuana behavior as demonstrated by earlier research. During the pilot studies items 35-38 were developed to measure time orientation. The measures of marijuana behavior used in the analyses presented in this book were based on whether marijuana had ever been used, and the recency and frequency of marijuana use (Appendix A, Questions 9 and 12).

REFERENCES

Glenn, William A., and Louise G. Richards. Recent Surveys of Nonmedical Drug Use: A Compendium of Abstracts. Rockville, Md.: National Institute on Drug Abuse, 1974.

McLeod, Jonnie H., and Gloria A. Grizzle. Alcohol and Other Drug Usage among Junior and Senior High School Students in Charlotte-Mecklenburg. Chapel Hill, N.C.: Institute of Government, 1974.

Nehemkis, Alexis, Mary A. Macari, and Dan J. Lettieri. Drug Abuse Instrument Handbook (Research Issues 12), DHEW Publication No. (ADM) 76-394. Washington, D.C.: Government Printing Office, 1976.

U.S. Bureau of the Census. General Social and Economic Characteristics, Final Report PC(1)-C-35, North Carolina. Washington, D.C.: Government Printing Office, 1972, Table 43.

3
DATA COLLECTION

IDENTIFICATION OF SUBJECTS
ELIGIBLE FOR ROUND 1

The process of gathering data from subjects the first time is referred to as Round 1. In preparation for Round 1, during the last week of January and the first week of February 1976, the researchers obtained the names and addresses of parents of all seventh graders enrolled in the eight schools. Three of the schools provided lists containing this information, and the research staff copied the data from student cards maintained by the five other schools. The 2,370 students identified as prospective subjects are distributed by school in the first column of Table 3.1.

As a crude check to be sure that significant numbers of students were not inadvertently excluded from these lists, the number of students on the lists (Column 1 of Table 3.1) were compared with the tallies of seventh graders at the beginning of the school year (Column 2 of Table 3.1). Perfect agreement was not expected because a net change in enrollment had, in all likelihood, occurred during this time. However, moderate differences would signal the need to question whether all students eligible for study had been identified. The greatest discrepancy was for East Garner, with 286 students enrolled at the beginning of the school year and 268 identified for the study. Each entry on the list for East Garner was checked with the file at the school and they were found to coincide perfectly. Apparently the lists had excluded very few, if any, eligible subjects.

TABLE 3.1

Number of Students Identified for Study and Enrolled at
Beginning of School Year, by School

School	Number of Students Identified as Prospective Subjects	Number of Students Enrolled at Beginning of School Year
East Garner	268	286
North Garner	310	318
Fuquay-Varina	210	210
Wake Forest	255	247
Millbrook	359	353
East Cary	332	327
West Cary	347	361
East Millbrook	289	295
Total*	2,370	2,397

*There was a net loss of 27 students between the time the
schools made their count of enrollment at the beginning of the
school year and the time lists for the study were compiled.

INFORMING PARENTS ABOUT THE STUDY

When the questionnaire and data-collection procedures in the
two Chapel Hill/Carrboro junior high schools were being piloted,
letters were sent to the parents of 212 seventh graders to inform
them about the study and to request that they consider giving permission for the participation of their children in the pilot. Only 35
percent of the parents returned letters to grant consent. A telephone survey was conducted with a random sample of 50 of those
who did not return the letter giving consent, in order to learn what
might be done to improve the letter and procedure for future stages
of the research. The letter in Appendix C reflects what was learned
from those parents.

The letter in Appendix C was mailed to the parents of the
2,370 prospective subjects. The purposes of the letter were to inform parents about the study and to give them the opportunity to
deny permission for their children's participation. Letters for 34
parents were repeatedly returned by the U.S. Postal Service for
having incorrect addresses, and it was never possible to identify
correct addresses for these parents. Their children were declared
ineligible for study.

Letters were returned by 872 (37 percent) of the parents. Of these, 743 (85 percent) gave signed permission for their children's participation in the research. These children, plus those whose parents did not deny consent, were declared eligible for the study. Of those who returned letters, 129 (15 percent) indicated that they did not want their children to participate, and these children were excluded from the study.

Ten parents responded to the invitation to call the project director for additional information, a few directed inquiries to the schools, and several inspected the questionnaires that had been placed at the schools. Overall, among the parents who contacted the research office or the schools by telephone or personal visit, approximately eight out of ten were favorably inclined toward the study.

ADMINISTERING THE QUESTIONNAIRE

Round 1 data gathering in the schools began on March 9, 1976 and ended April 21, 1976. The physical facilities of the schools determined where the questionnaires were administered. Sessions were held in gymnasiums, cafeterias, auditoriums, or large classrooms. In all sessions there was sufficient room for the students to spread out in order to minimize joint consideration of the questionnaire and the observation of responses recorded by others. Two members of the research team were primarily responsible for administering questionnaires, often with the assistance of other team members. In all sessions a guidance counselor or teacher from the school was present. The number of students in each session ranged from 30 to 90, with most sessions including about 50 students. All sessions lasted two school periods, usually for a total of 90 minutes.

The first three minutes of each session were devoted to making certain no students ineligible for participation were in the room, such as students whose parents had denied consent, students whose parents had not been contacted about the study because they had enrolled after the lists of subjects had been compiled, and children whose parents were believed not to have received the letter.

The next ten minutes were spent providing students with detailed information about the study. The Information Form (Appendix D) was read and discussed with the students to guide this process. Two aspects of the introduction need to be mentioned. First, at least twice during each introduction it was strongly emphasized that students should feel completely free not to participate and that there would be no repercussions of any kind if that was their decision. Second, an explanation was made to the students of the need for a record of their names, and of the procedures being used to assure confidentiality. Students were told not to record their names on questionnaires. Each subject was asked to write her or his name on a slip of paper that bore a unique number matching a number on the questionnaire. In this way the Round 1 and Round 2 questionnaires could later be linked and questionnaires and names could be kept separate. These slips of paper were placed in a locked box by the students before completing the questionnaire, and the students were informed the box would be deposited with the Institute for Research in Social Science at the university. They were assured that the Institute would not have access to the information on the questionnaires, and that no member of the research team would have access to the slips with the names and numbers. In this way no one could match a name with a questionnaire. While safeguarding names of subjects, the Institute could provide numbers to link Round 1 questionnaires with those to be completed during Round 2. This procedure was developed during pilot studies, and made sure that subjects understood the procedure and knew that their responses would be confidential, thus encouraging the honesty of responses to the questions.

The pilot study questionnaire began with a one-item test to identify subjects who were unaware of marijuana. This test was included because of the questionnaire would not be understood by a person who had not heard of marijuana, and a substantial number of parents had suggested their children did not know what marijuana is. All of our 200 pilot subjects passed the exam and therefore we deleted the item for Round 1. However, after students agreed to participate by signing the Information Form they were shown a sign containing the word "marijuana," and the word was pronounced several times to make certain everyone recognized the word which was used frequently in the questionnaire. Then, using a large visual aid (Appendix B), the research assistant devoted an average of ten minutes to a verbal explanation on how to complete the section of the questionnaire designed to measure anticipated consequences, salience, and subjective probability (Appendix A). The remaining time, ranging from 30 to 60 minutes among subjects, was devoted to completing the questionnaire.

REASONS FOR NONCOMPLETION OF
QUESTIONNAIRE, ROUND 1

A total of 1,686 or 71 percent of the 2,370 prospective subjects completed the first questionnaire. The first column of Table 3.2 provides information for those prospective subjects who did not

complete the Round 1 questionnaire. Note that the figures indicate
the percentage only of subjects who did not complete questionnaires
and not of the 2,370 on the initial list of prospective subjects.
Among those not completing the questionnaire the largest category
contained those who decided not to participate when the study was
being introduced to them at school (34 percent). The only criticism
of the procedures received from school personnel—and this was
made at several schools—was that had the voluntary nature of the
study not been emphasized so strongly, then few if any children
would have left a session. However, this procedure was continued
in order to assure that the students felt no obligation to participate.
Of those not completing questionnaires, 23 percent were absent
from school when the questionnaire was being administered. Parents denied consent for 19 percent of those who did not complete
questionnaires. For 5 percent of these prospective subjects the
letters were returned after repeated mailings with updated addresses, and since it was not certain that the parents were informed
about the study, these children were not allowed to participate. Another 19 percent did not complete the questionnaire for a variety of
other reasons; for example, some had moved from the school system before field work began, or the schools considered the participation of some to be impossible due to severe reading disabilities.

TABLE 3.2

Classification of Nonparticipating Prospective Subjects
According to Reasons for Nonparticipation
(percent)

Reason for Nonparticipation	Round 1 N = 684	Round 2 N = 404	Total N = 1,088
Parent did not return letter indicating consent	0	66.7	24.8
Subject did not consent	34.5	3.2	22.9
Absent from school	23.0	5.7	16.5
Parent denied consent	18.8	12.6	16.5
Other	19.0	0	11.9
Known to have moved from the area	0	10.6	4.0
Insufficient address	4.7	1.2	3.4
Total	100.0	100.0	100.0

The percentage completing Round 1 questionnaires was substantially less than was expected before data collection. One reason was that it had been planned to continue returning to the schools until all absentees had been given the opportunity to participate. This had just begun when data collection was suspended as a result of concern about the procedures used for informed consent and confidentiality.

PROBLEMS WITH INFORMED CONSENT
AND CONFIDENTIALITY

On April 21, 1976, while data were being collected from subjects who had been absent from school when the questionnaire had been administered earlier, and while the questionnaire was being administered to some children a second time so that test-retest reliability could be assessed, the research staff was informed that administrative officials of the university had ordered immediate suspension of all work on the research. They had three objections to the procedures.

First, the letter informing parents of the study (Appendix C), should have stated explicitly that the subjects would be asked if they used drugs, and should have named some of the drugs the students would be asked about. Second, only children whose parents returned a signed letter granting permission for participation should have been included in the study. These subjects had been included, plus children whose parents received the letter and did not deny consent. Third, the children were asked to report illegal behavior. A court of law could subpoena the data, and contempt charges could be levied unless the court were given the data. The data were to be destroyed and the research terminated unless these problems could be resolved. Prior to using these procedures, approval had been received from the Institutional Review Board for the Protection of Human Subjects.

The research was at a standstill during the ten months required to solve the final problem. The first and second objections, related to informed consent, were removed when the researchers agreed to send a new letter to all parents prior to Round 2 (Appendix E) and to include in the study only those children whose parents returned a signed letter indicating permission for their participation in Round 2 and permission for the research team to use the data collected in Round 1. The data collected from children whose parents did not give signed permission could not be used in any way. Several methods for protecting the data from subpoena and effective contempt charges were considered, including data storage outside the United States. The only legally effective and methodologically acceptable mechanism identified was a grant of confidentiality from the U.S. Department of Health, Education and Welfare, as authorized under Section 303(a) of the Public Health Service Act (U.S. Congress, 1970). That was granted ten months after the initial request.

These events had a number of effects on the research and may have biased the results. It was estimated that a minimum 78 percent of the sample would have completed Round 1 questionnaires rather than 71 percent, if it had been possible to follow up on prospective subjects who were absent the days the questionnaires were administered. Moreover, when the data collection was interrupted, the researchers were in the process of having 250 subjects complete the questionnaire a second time for the purpose of assessing the test-retest reliability of the measures. It was possible to obtain reliability checks for only a few cases when ordered to stop data collection, and therefore this assessment of measurement error could not be made.

ROUND 2 DATA COLLECTION

Of the 1,686 subjects who completed Round 1 questionnaires, 33 were eliminated because the institute was unable to link the slips containing their names and questionnaire identification numbers with the master list of subjects. Thus, Round 2 began with 1,653 prospective participants.

The revised informed consent letter (Appendix E) was mailed to the parents of these 1,653 children during the first week of April 1977. Two weeks later, and continuing for four weeks, four full-time research assistants telephoned parents who had not responded to the letter to answer any questions they had about the study. Letters were returned by 1,379 (83 percent) of the parents, and of these, 1,285 (93 percent) gave permission for their children to participate in the study.

Six parents responded to the invitation to call the project director for additional information about the research. Three of the calls indicated a positive feeling about the research. Of the remaining three, one parent called to say they had moved from the study area, and two expressed their concerns about negative effects the study might have for the child. These latter two parents were advised not to give permission for the participation of their children.

The data collection procedures for Round 2 were essentially the same as described for Round 1 except that four items designed to measure religion and the education of parents were deleted from the questionnaire. This deletion was required by the school system that consolidated with the school system in this study between Rounds 1 and 2.

Of the 1,285 children whose parents gave permission for Round 2 participation, 1,249 (97 percent) completed questionnaires between May 23 and June 7, 1977.

REASONS FOR NONCOMPLETION OF QUESTIONNAIRE, ROUND 2

The study began with 2,370 prospective subjects. A total of 1,290 (54.4 percent) completed Round 1 and Round 2 questionnaires; 684 did not complete Round 1 questionnaires and 404 who completed Round 1 questionnaires did not complete Round 2 questionnaires.

Most of the prospective Round 2 subjects who did not complete questionnaires had parents who did not return the letter indicating their consent for participation (66.7 percent). Parents denied consent for 12.6 percent of the subjects who did not complete the second questionnaire, and at least 10.6 percent of those not completing the questionnaire had moved from the study area. Less than 10 percent of those not participating in Round 2 were children who decided against participation, who were absent from school when questionnaires were administered, or for whom information on their home addresses was incomplete and therefore the informed consent letter could not be sent.

Overall, for both rounds, as indicated in the total column of Table 3.2, the most common reason for not participating in the study was that the parent did not return the letter giving consent for participation (24.8 percent). Of those not participating in either Round 1 or 2, 22.9 percent were subjects who chose not to participate. Being absent from school when the questionnaire was being administered accounted for 16.5 percent of the nonparticipants. A total of 16.5 percent of the nonparticipants had parents who denied consent. Fewer than 4 percent did not participate either because they moved from the area or had an insufficient address, and 12 percent of the nonparticipants did not complete questionnaires for other reasons.

Of the 1,290 cases who completed Round 1 and Round 2 questionnaires, 88 were deleted because their Round 1 and Round 2 questionnaires could not be linked. Also deleted were an additional 124 cases who had missing information on one or more of the key variables of the study as measured in either Round 1 or Round 2. These 124 cases are distributed according to reason for deletion in

Table 3.3 The criterion for deleting cases because of inadequate information on salience and subjective probability is described in Appendix F. Thus, most of the analyses to be presented are based on a sample of 1,078 that represents 45.5 percent of the 2,370 cases eligible for study at the outset.

TABLE 3.3

Cases Deleted Due to Missing Information,
by Reason for Deletion

Reason for Deletion	Number of Cases
Insufficient information on salience and/or subjective probability to measure utility structure	60
Missing information on time orientation	10
Unknown if marijuana had ever been used	19
Indicated marijuana had been used on Round 1 questionnaire, and that marijuana had never been used on Round 2 questionnaire	11
Recency or frequency of marijuana use unknown	24
Total	124

SAMPLE ATTRITION AND BIAS

Many students initially selected for study are not represented in the analyses presented. This attrition could have influenced the findings if those who did not provide information differed substantially from those who did. For example, if respondents and non-respondents differ with respect to their use of marijuana, then the marijuana behavior of the 1,078 subjects does not reflect the behavior of the 2,370 students originally eligible for study. Associations between variables could also be biased by attrition. For example, a relationship between the utility structure and marijuana behavior for all the students might not be the same for the students represented in the data. Little comfort is gained from the fact that the attrition rate in this study is less than exists in many other longitudinal studies of drug behavior (Kandel 1978), even though the comparability of these studies might be enhanced by similarly high rates of attrition.

Unfortunately, there is no acceptable way to assess bias attributable to attrition in this study because that would require information from both nonrespondents and respondents. There were questionnaires from a substantial number of subjects who completed Round 1 questionnaires but not Round 2 questionnaires, and a comparison of them with respect to their Round 1 measures, and correlations among variables within these two groups, could have shed some light on the question of bias due to attrition. However, in order to continue the study it was necessary to agree not to use the data from subjects who provided Round 1 data unless parental permission was given to use those data and the information collected in Round 2. Thus, this comparison could not be made. It might have been possible to obtain crude estimates of attrition bias by comparing the data in the final sample with information collected in the school located in the study locale that participated in the pilot study with very low attrition, but the researchers had to agree not to use the pilot data in order to salvage the study. Thus, it is not possible to use the data to gauge the effects attrition might have had for the results.

There have been numerous studies of the influence of attrition on bias, many of which are identified in Dalenius (1971). In general, these studies indicate that attrition does produce at least moderate bias for a wide variety of measures. Earlier studies of attrition bias in studies of drug behavior suggest a number of correlates of attrition that might influence results (Josephson and Rosen 1978). The attrition in these studies appears to be predominantly for reasons other than a failure to have parents return an informed consent form for their child's participation, the major source of attrition in this study, and therefore their findings are not directly comparable. One study has assessed attrition bias attributable to informed consent procedures (Lueptow et al. 1977) and found minimal bias even though there was substantial attrition.

It appears, then, that there is no adequate way to assess bias that might be present in the data as a result of attrition. The best that can be done is to assume that there may be bias, and to restrict generalization of the findings to populations that would be similarly selective with respect to participation.

REFERENCES

Dalenius, Tore. Bibliography on Non-sampling Errors (Preliminary Version). Stockholm: Institute of Statistics, 1971.

Josephson, Eric, and Matthew A. Rosen. "Panel Loss in a High
School Drug Study." In Longitudinal Research on Drug Use:
Empirical Findings and Methodological Issues, edited by Denise
B. Kandel, pp. 115-33. Washington, D.C.: Hemisphere Pub-
lishing Corporation, 1978.

Kandel, Denise B. "Convergences in Prospective Longitudinal Surveys of Drug Use in Normal Populations." In Longitudinal Research on Drug Use: Empirical Findings and Methodological
Issues, edited by Denise B. Kandel, pp. 6-11. Washington,
D.C.: Hemisphere Publishing Corporation, 1978.

Lueptow, Lloyd, et al. "The Impact of Informed Consent Regula-
tions on Response Rate and Response Bias." Sociological
Methods and Research 6 (1977): 183-204.

U.S. Congress, Public Law 91-513 (Comprehensive Drug Abuse
Prevention and Control Act of 1970), 84 STAT., 1241, October
27, 1970.

4
CHARACTERS OF THE SAMPLE

This chapter describes the study participants according to several demographic characteristics, their reported use of marijuana, and the consequences they anticipated from use of marijuana as indicated on the Round 1 questionnaires.

DEMOGRAPHIC CHARACTERISTICS

The distributions of sample members according to selected demographic variables are shown in Table 4.1. In the sample, 87.9 percent are white and 42.7 percent are male; 39 percent are 12 years of age and 54.7 percent are 13 years of age. Nearly half of the subjects have fathers with education beyond high school.

USE OF MARIJUANA

Table 4.2 shows the distribution of the sample according to their use of marijuana as indicated on the Round 1 and Round 2 questionnaires. A total of 749 (70.4 percent) reported on both questionnaires that they had never used marijuana. On Round 1 questionnaires, 188 (17.4 percent) indicated that they had never used marijuana, but reported on their Round 2 questionnaires that they had used marijuana. A total of 131 (12.2 percent) reported on both questionnaires that they had used marijuana.

Viewing these data a little differently, 12.2 percent had used marijuana near the end of their seventh grade of school, and 29.6 percent [(188 + 131) / 1078] had used marijuana by the time their eighth grade in school was almost completed. These percents for the participants in the study are higher than reported in a national survey in 1976. In the national study, 6 percent of those aged 12-13

TABLE 4.1

Selected Characteristics of Sample

Characteristic	Percent	Number
Race		
White	87.9	948
Nonwhite	12.1	130
Total	100.0	1,078
Sex		
Male	42.7	460
Female	57.3	618
Total	100.0	1,078
Age[a]		
<12	0.6	5
12	38.8	418
13	54.7	590
>13	5.9	64
Total	100.0	1,077
Father's education[b]		
<High school	14.4	149
High school	20.6	213
>High school	47.9	494
Don't know	17.1	177
Total	100.0	1,033

[a]One case not included due to missing information.
[b]45 cases not included due to missing information.

TABLE 4.2

Use of Marijuana
(N = 1,078)

Response		Percent	Number
Round 1	Round 2		
Never use	Never use	70.4	759
Never use	Use	17.4	188
Use	Use	12.2	131

45

TABLE 4.3

Percent of Positive Attributes Chosen
on Round 1 by Round 1 Use

Attribute	Nonusers N = 947	Users N = 131	t
Get high	44.0	80.9	9.69[a]
Have other kids think that I am cool	26.1	29.8	.87
Feel as if time were passing slower	11.5	16.8	1.54
Have more self-confidence	17.4	20.6	.85
Be able to do things better	8.7	13.7	1.61
Feel more pleasure	39.6	79.4	10.23[a]
Feel closer to others	12.3	23.7	2.94[a]
Enjoy doing things with my friends	19.6	44.3	5.42[a]
Feel stronger	13.7	14.5	.24
Enjoy the taste	15.4	35.1	4.53[a]
Understand myself better	9.9	17.6	2.20[b]
Act against my parents, other adults or society	17.1	16.8	.09
Feel at home with the group	25.2	39.7	3.20[a]
See, smell, taste, hear or feel things better	7.2	13.0	1.89
Be less bored	34.9	61.1	5.77[a]
Have less pain	20.4	38.2	3.99[a]
Worry less	50.6	67.2	3.75[a]
Have different or interesting thoughts	20.9	27.5	1.59
Feel more important or grown-up	17.5	18.3	.22
Sleep better	12.9	31.3	4.37[a]
Feel happier	40.9	71.0	7.02[a]
Be able to think better	6.8	7.6	.35
Be more relaxed	35.4	67.2	7.22[a]
Help me control my weight	5.1	4.6	.25
Satisfy my curiosity	37.7	36.6	.23
Be liked more by my friends or have more friends	15.6	24.4	2.23[b]

[a] $p < .01.$

[b] $p < .05.$

TABLE 4.4

Percent of Negative Attributes Chosen
on Round 1 by Round 1 Use

Attribute	Nonusers N = 947	Users N = 131	t
Be arrested by the police	84.3	87.0	.87
Be a bad example for others	68.9	32.8	8.22[a]
Do strange or dangerous things, lose control over myself	81.7	45.8	7.90[a]
Not live as long	43.4	20.6	5.85[a]
Feel like I am going crazy	63.8	27.5	8.61[a]
Be less understanding of myself	31.9	13.0	5.71[a]
Not be able to think as well	66.2	38.2	6.19[a]
Become more nervous	47.3	22.1	6.31[a]
Get into trouble with parents	76.9	64.9	2.72[a]
Cause accidents	64.1	32.8	7.10[a]
Go on to more harmful drugs	78.5	46.5	6.97[a]
Be sadder	21.1	7.6	5.03[a]
Lose interest in things	39.0	22.1	4.24[a]
Not be able to do things such as running or walking as well	48.1	29.8	4.22[a]
Go to jail	72.1	64.1	1.80
Feel as if time were passing slower	17.3	12.2	1.63
Be liked less by friends or have fewer friends	47.2	19.1	7.38[a]
Feel guilty because it is against the law, or against my religion, or against my morals	51.7	19.9	8.27[a]
Feel bad	66.4	25.9	9.77[a]
Get into trouble with the teacher or principal	51.7	42.0	2.11[b]
Get into trouble with people who sell drugs	52.3	29.8	5.20[a]
Have to spend too much money	45.1	42.0	.67
Get into trouble with the police	75.7	61.8	3.10[a]
Harm my body forever	60.9	25.2	8.66[a]
Lose respect for myself	40.8	16.8	6.57[a]
Dislike the taste	14.8	4.6	4.71[a]
Not be able to stop using drugs	79.2	38.9	9.00[a]
Die from an overdose	71.0	36.6	7.67[a]

[a] $p < .01.$
[b] $p < .05.$

47

and 21 percent of those aged 14–15, which corresponds crudely to the seventh and eighth grade levels, had used marijuana (National Institute on Drug Abuse 1976).

ANTICIPATED CONSEQUENCES

The percentages of students selecting the consequences during Round 1 according to their use of marijuana are shown in Table 4.3 for the positive consequences and Table 4.4 for the negative consequences. The variation in percentages by attribute is substantial. And, as would be expected from the theory, those who had and had not used marijuana differ substantially: comparing these groups for many of the consequences, users are relatively likely to identify positive consequences, and nonusers are relatively likely to select negative consequences. These data are shown to provide a description of the sample. However, it is not possible to determine from the data in these tables whether the imbalance of positive and negative consequences influences, or is influenced by, behavior with marijuana. Moreover, those results ignore components of the utility structure other than the attribute. The analyses presented in the next chapter were conducted to test the hypothesis that the utility structure predicts subsequent use of marijuana.

REFERENCE

National Institute on Drug Abuse. Marijuana and Health. Sixth Annual Report to the U.S. Congress from the Secretary of Health, Education and Welfare. 1976 DHEW Publication No. (ADM) 77–443. Washington, D.C.: Government Printing Office, 1977.

5
THE UTILITY STRUCTURE OF NONUSERS AND THEIR SUBSEQUENT USE OF MARIJUANA

This chapter presents the analyses conducted to determine whether the data are consistent with the hypothesis that the utility structure influences the use of marijuana. Only the 947 subjects who indicated on their Round 1 questionnaires that they had never used marijuana are considered, and their utility structures as measured in Round 1 are related to their use of marijuana as indicated by Round 2. By omitting those who reported on their Round 1 questionnaires that they had used marijuana, it is possible to eliminate from this analysis the possible influence of use of marijuana upon the utility structure. The dependent variable is the use of marijuana by Round 2. Also presented are the analyses conducted to determine whether all components of the utility structure are necessary for predicting behavior with marijuana. The method of generating a measure of the utility structure for each subject is described.

THE UTILITY STRUCTURE INDEX

The utility structure index created includes all the components: attribute, salience, subjective probability, delayed consequence, and time orientation. Each individual is assigned a value on the index that represents the degree to which relative good or harm is expected from using marijuana. In composing the index, the positive consequences are considered first. Each positive attribute selected by the subject on the first page of the questionnaire (Appendix A) was scored 1, and each positive attribute not chosen was scored zero. The measure of salience for each attribute is from the second part of the questionnaire (Appendix A), and ranged from 1 to 5 with 5 indicating high salience. The measure of subjective probability for each attribute is from the third part of the questionnaire (Appendix A), and ranges from 1 to 5, with 5 indicating high subjective probability.

Delayed consequence and time orientation were treated as follows. The research team derived a consensus opinion regarding which of the attributes would be perceived as accruing during or soon after marijuana use (immediate), and which of the attributes would accrue later (delayed). The results of that consensus are indicated in Table 5.1. Each of the four time orientation items in the questionnaire (see Items 35 to 38, Appendix A) was coded to range from 1 to 4, with a score of 4 indicating present orientation. The scores for the four items were then summed for each subject. The distribution on this time orientation scale for subjects who indicated on their Round 1 questionnaire that they had never used marijuana is shown in Table 5.2. Each positive attribute classified as immediate was multiplied by the individual's score on time orientation. The scores on time orientation were reversed when dealing with delayed consequences. For example, subjects in the most future-oriented category were assigned a score of 16, and those in the most present-oriented category were assigned a score of 4. Each positive attribute classified as delayed was then multiplied by the subject's score on this variable. This adjustment of immediate and delayed consequences for time orientation gives increased weight to the immediate consequences chosen by present-oriented individuals, relatively little weight to the future consequences chosen by present-oriented individuals, increased weight to the future consequences chosen by future-oriented individuals, and relatively little weight to the immediate consequences chosen by future-oriented individuals. The weighting of immediate and delayed consequences for time orientation is called "time."

For each attribute and subject the products of the attribute, salience, subjective probability, and time scores described in the preceding two paragraphs were calculated. These products were then summed for all positive consequences for each case. Scores for the negative consequences and components were created in a manner identical to that described for the positive consequences, yielding a sum of the negative consequences for each subject. The utility structure index was then calculated for each subject by subtracting the sum of the negative scores from the sum of the positive scores. Thus, each subject was given a single value on the index which reflects all components of the utility structure, and represents the degree to which more benefit or harm is expected from marijuana.

Some subjects skipped items necessary to derive their measures of utility structures. For some of these cases the missing values were estimated from other information they supplied. The procedures for doing this are described in Appendix F.

TABLE 5.1

Designation of Immediate and Delayed Consequences

Positive		Negative	
Immediate	Delayed	Immediate	Delayed
Get high	Be able to think better	Be arrested by the police	Not live as long
Have other kids think that I am cool	Help me control my weight	Be a bad example for others	Not be able to think as well
Feel as if time were passing slower		Do strange or dangerous things, lose control over myself	Go on to more harmful drugs
Have more self-confidence		Feel like I am going crazy	Lose interest in things
Be able to do things better		Be less understanding of myself	Be liked less by friends or have fewer friends
Feel more pleasure		Become more nervous	Get into trouble with people who sell drugs
Feel closer to others		Get into trouble with parents	Have to spend too much money
Enjoy doing things with my friends		Cause accidents	Harm my body forever
Feel stronger		Be sadder	Not be able to stop using drugs
Enjoy the taste		Not be able to do things such as running or walking as well	
Understand myself better		Go to jail	
Act against my parents, other adults or society		Feel as if time were passing slower	
Feel at home with the group		Feel guilty because it is against the law, or because it is against my religion, or because it is against my morals	
See, smell, taste, hear or feel things better		Feel bad	
Be less bored		Get into trouble with the teacher or principal	
Have less pain		Get into trouble with the police	
Worry less		Lose respect for myself	
Have different or interesting thoughts		Dislike the taste	
Feel more important or grown-up		Die from an overdose	
Sleep better			
Feel happier			
Be more relaxed			
Satisfy my curiosity			
Be liked more by my friends or have more friends			

TABLE 5.2

Distribution on Time Orientation Scale as Measured in Round 1
(Sample: Nonusers, Round 1)

Time Orientation	Number of Cases
16 (most present-oriented)	2
13	12
12	12
11	19
10	52
9	90
8	110
7	159
6	228
5	134
4 (most future-oriented)	129
Total	947

RELATIONSHIP BETWEEN UTILITY
STRUCTURE AND BEHAVIOR

Table 5.3 shows a cross tabulation of the Round 1 utility structure index with Round 2 use of marijuana for subjects who said during Round 1 that they had never used marijuana. The cutting points
for the utility structure index in Table 5.3 were established by
using the criterion that each cell contain a minimum expected frequency of 5 so that the chi-square test could be used, and as many
categories as possible could be used to avoid obscuring relationships. In Table 5.3, marijuana use increases in a generally linear
fashion as the utility structure becomes more positive. The relationship is quite striking: the percent of users ranges from less
than 10 percent among those with the more negative utility structures, to 56.8 percent among those with the most positive utility
structures. This relationship is in the hypothesized direction and
statistically significant (chi-square = 70.8, $p < .0001$; contingency
coefficient = .26).

TABLE 5.3

Utility Structure Index as Measured in Round 1,
by Use in Round 2
(Sample: Nonusers, Round 1)

	Users, Round 2	
Utility Structure Index	Percent	Number
-100 to -149	56.8	44
-150 to -299	29.4	34
-300 to -449	37.0	46
-450 to -599	16.7	54
-600 to -749	16.7	66
-750 to -899	23.1	52
-900 to -1049	17.2	64
-1050 to -1199	23.4	64
-1200 to -1349	23.8	80
-1350 to -1499	16.7	65
-1500 to -1649	19.2	53
-1650 to -1799	23.2	56
-1800 to -1949	10.5	38
-1950 to -2099	8.5	47
-2100 to -2249	7.0	43
-2250 to -3450	9.9	141
Total	19.9	947

Note: Chi-square = 70.8, $p < .0001$; contingency coefficient = .26.

CONTRIBUTIONS OF THE COMPONENTS

This section presents the analyses that were conducted to identify the relative contributions to behavior of the components of the utility structure. Said somewhat differently, the question addressed here is whether all the components of the utility structure index are necessary for explaining marijuana use, and if not, which are the important components. This is of both theoretical and practical significance. The theory would be carrying excess baggage if some of the components are unnecessary for explaining behavior. Thus, for the sake of parsimony, it is of value to reduce the number of components if possible. The components analysis could also have practical significance. For example, if salience is an essential ingredient of the utility structure but subjective probability is not, then perhaps subjective probability need not be emphasized in education programs. That would be a marked departure from most current programs that emphasize the risks associated with behavior. If time is a critical ingredient but subjective probability is not, then the present orientation to drug education programs may be improperly focused, and the programs should be directed toward assessing the individual's time orientation and the immediate and future characteristics of the consequences of marijuana use.

First, seven indexes were created for each subject, representing varying combinations of the components. These were calculated as follows:

1. Attribute Index. Each positive and negative attribute chosen was scored 1, and each attribute not chosen was scored zero. The positive and negative attribute scores were summed separately for each case. The attribute index for each case is the sum of the negative scores subtracted from the sum of the positive scores.

2. Attribute-Salience Index. Each positive and negative attribute chosen was scored 1, and each attribute not chosen was scored zero. The salience scores from the questionnaire, ranging from 1 to 5, with 5 indicating high salience, were multiplied by their companion attribute scores. The positive and negative products were summed separately for each case. The attribute-salience index for each case is the sum of the negative products subtracted from the sum of the positive products.

3. Attribute-Subjective Probability Index. Each positive and negative attribute chosen was scored 1, and each attribute not chosen was scored zero. The subjective probability scores from the questionnaire, ranging from 1 to 5, with 5 indicating high subjective probability, were multiplied by their companion attribute scores. The positive and negative attribute products were summed separately for each case. The attribute-subjective probability index for each case is the sum of the negative products subtracted from the sum of the positive products.

4. Attribute-Time Index. Each positive and negative attribute chosen was scored 1, and each attribute not chosen was scored zero. The time scores described in the preceding section were multiplied by their companion attribute scores. The positive and negative attribute products were summed separately for each case. The attribute-time index for each case is the sum of the negative products subtracted from the sum of the positive products.

5. Attribute-Salience-Subjective Probability Index. Each attribute chosen was scored 1, and each attribute not chosen was scored zero. The salience and subjective probability scores were multiplied by their companion attribute scores. The positive and negative attribute products were summed separately for each case. The attribute-salience-subjective probability index for each case is the sum of the negative products subtracted from the sum of the positive products.

6. Attribute-Salience-Time Index. Each attribute chosen was scored 1, and each attribute not chosen was scored zero. The salience and time scores were multiplied by their companion attribute scores. The positive and negative attribute products were summed separately for each case. The attribute-salience-time index for each case is the sum of the negative products subtracted from the sum of the positive products.

7. Attribute-Subjective Probability-Time Index. Each attribute chosen was scored 1, and each attribute not chosen was scored zero. The subjective probability and time scores were multiplied by their companion attribute scores. The positive and negative attribute products were summed separately for each case. The attribute-subjective probability-time index for each case is the sum of the negative products subtracted from the sum of the positive products.

In addition, in this analysis the utility structure index described in the preceding section was used, which includes all components.

Six regression analyses were conducted, with marijuana use as the dependent variable, to identify the components necessary for explaining use of marijuana. As in preceding analyses, only those subjects were included who had never used marijuana by Round 1 and the Round 1 indexes were related to Round 2 use. The results, which are described in the next paragraph, are shown in Table 5.4. In each of the six regression analyses, the attribute index was entered as the first independent variable because all the other components depend upon the attribute measure for measurement, and therefore if only one component were sufficient, it would be that one. In the second step of the regressions the two-component combinations were added. That is, after entering the attribute index, attribute-salience, attribute-subjective probability, or attribute-time were then added. Next, each of the possible three-component indexes, which included a component not present in the preceding step, were entered. For example, when the attribute index was entered first and attribute-salience second, one regression was conducted in which attribute-salience-subjective probability was added third (Analysis 1) and another in which attribute-salience-time was

TABLE 5.4

Regression Analyses of Selected Combinations of Components as Measured
in Round 1 with Order of Entry Predetermined

(Sample: Nonusers, Round 1; Dependent Variable: Use, Round 2; N = 947)

	Analysis Number										
	1		2		3		4		5		6
Order of entry:	F	Order of entry:	F	Order of entry:	F	Order of entry:	F	Order of entry:	F	Order of entry:	F
Attribute	36.4*	Attribute	36.4*	Attribute	36.4*	Attribute	36.4*	Attribute	36.4*	Attribute	36.4*
Attribute-salience	.0	Attribute-salience	.0	Attribute-subjective probability	13.8*	Attribute-subjective probability	13.8*	Attribute-time	.9	Attribute-time	.9
Attribute-salience-subjective probability	15.7*	Attribute-salience-time	2.2	Attribute-subjective probability-salience	3.1	Attribute-subjective probability-time	.5	Attribute-time-salience	.0	Attribute-time-subjective probability	13.3*
Attribute-salience-subjective probability-time	1.9	Attribute-salience-subjective probability-time	14.6*	Attribute-salience-subjective probability-time	2.0	Attribute-salience-subjective probability-time	1.8	Attribute-salience-subjective probability-time	14.2*	Attribute-salience-subjective probability-time	2.1

*p < .01 by $\underline{F}$ test.

entered third (Analysis 2). Finally, as the final step in each regression, the utility structure index was added, since it contains
all components.

As indicated in Table 5.4, the attribute index explains a statistically significant amount of variance in marijuana use ($\underline{F}$ = 36.4,
p < .01). Use increases as the index becomes more positive. In all
six analyses, statistically significant increases in variance explained,
beyond that accounted for by the attribute alone, were found only
when the subjective probability component was added. In each analysis, when subjective probability was added at either the second or
third step (Analyses 1, 3, 4, and 6), addition of components after
subjective probability did not increase the variance explained by a
statistically significant amount. Note Analyses 3 and 4 in particular. When subjective probability was entered as the second step, a
statistically significant increase in variance was explained, but addition of time and salience did not add to the explanation of marijuana
use. It is concluded that the components salience and time do not
add to the explanation of marijuana use, subjective probability does
add explained variance, and therefore the attribute-subjective probability index is sufficient.

It is not concluded from this analysis that the other indexes
are unrelated to use of marijuana. Indeed, there is a statistically
significant relationship in the hypothesized direction between marijuana use and each index as shown in Table 5.5. This is not surprising, given the strong correlations among the indexes shown in
Table 5.6. Many of the correlations in Table 5.6 are so strong that
the use of regression for the components analysis may not be completely appropriate as a result of collinearity. In any case it appears that each of the indexes appears to be an acceptable substitute
for any other index. Further, the components analysis suggests
that the addition of time and salience to the attribute-subjective
probability index does not increase the explanation of use of marijuana by a statistically significant amount, and therefore the
attribute-subjective probability index, which has fewer components,
might just as well be used.

Table 5.7 shows a cross-tabulation of the Round 1 attribute-
subjective probability index with Round 2 use of marijuana for subjects who said during Round 1 that they had never used marijuana.
This is the same as Table 5.3, except that in Table 5.7 the attribute-
subjective probability index has been substituted for the utility structure index. The same criteria were used for establishing cutting
points of the indexes in Tables 5.3 and 5.7. The distributions in
Tables 5.3 and 5.7 are essentially the same. In Table 5.7, marijuana use increases as the attribute-subjective probability index becomes more positive, ranging from 10 percent or fewer users at the

negative end of the scale, to 55.8 percent toward the positive end. The relationship is in the hypothesized direction, generally linear, and statistically significant (chi-square = 73.7, p < .0001, contingency coefficient = .27).

TABLE 5.5

Differences between Round 2 Users and Nonusers
on Each Index
(Sample: Nonusers, Round 1)

Index	Mean for Round 2		t^*
	Users N = 188	Nonusers N = 759	
Attribute	-7.1	-10.6	6.2
Attribute-salience	-39.9	-55.0	5.7
Attribute-subjective probability	-28.8	-46.4	7.0
Attribute-time	-53.2	-72.8	6.0
Attribute-salience-subjective probability	-156.0	-232.5	6.4
Attribute-salience-time	-268.2	-355.8	5.8
Attribute-subjective probability-time	-205.5	-305.6	6.9
Attribute-salience-subjective probability-time	-1023.9	-1474.0	6.6

*Each t significant at p < .001.

There are many reasons why time and salience may have failed to add to the explanation of subsequent marijuana use in these data. Unfortunately, the data cannot be used to examine these reasons, but sketching several here may possibly provide guidance for future research. First, perhaps time and salience are simply unimportant components in a utility structure for explaining marijuana use. Most considerations of utility in field studies such as this do not break out the components to assess their relative effects, so one does not know whether the components were necessary for predicting behavior in the earlier studies. Secondly, perhaps the measures used here were insufficiently precise to tap the potential contributions of time and salience. It never seemed satisfactory to have the research team classify consequences as delayed and

TABLE 5.6

Correlation Matrix of Combinations of Components as Measured in Round 1
(Sample: Nonusers, Round 1; N = 947)

	Attribute	Attribute-Salience	Attribute-Subjective Probability	Attribute-Time	Attribute-Salience-Subjective Probability	Attribute-Salience-Time	Attribute-Subjective Probability-Time	Attribute-Salience-Subjective Probability-Time
Attribute	1.00	—	—	—	—	—	—	—
Attribute-salience	.95	1.00	—	—	—	—	—	—
Attribute-subjective probability	.94	.93	1.00	—	—	—	—	—
Attribute-time	.93	.93	.89	1.00	—	—	—	—
Attribute-salience-subjective probability	.88	.95	.97	.85	1.00	—	—	—
Attribute-salience-time	.88	.95	.88	.96	.91	1.00	—	—
Attribute-subjective probability-time	.87	.89	.95	.93	.94	.93	1.00	—
Attribute-salience-subjective probability-time	.82	.90	.92	.88	.96	.94	.98	1.00

Note: All correlations statistically significant at p < .001 (Pearson r).

immediate, and given more data collection time with each subject, they—the subjects—would have been asked to make this classification. Although the pilots of the salience measures suggested that the subjects understood the questions designed to assess this dimension, they still might have been too crude to add to the explanation in behavior. Third, perhaps salience and time were already taken into account by the subjects when they initially selected the consequences they expected from marijuana. If, for example, when considering peer approval and legal punishment as consequences of marijuana, the subjects were taking into account time and assessing importance as part of that judgment, then the salience and time measures would not be expected to add to the explanation of behavior.

TABLE 5.7

Attribute-Subjective Probability Index as Measured
in Round 1, by Use in Round 2
(Sample: Nonusers, Round 1)

| Attribute-Subjective | Users, Round 2 | |
Probability Index	Percent	Number
+ 30 to 0	55.8	43
0 to -5	41.9	43
-6 to -11	29.1	55
-12 to -17	22.2	63
-18 to -23	22.4	67
-24 to -29	13.0	77
-30 to -35	20.2	84
-36 to -41	21.1	90
-42 to -47	20.8	72
-48 to -53	14.3	56
-54 to -59	14.9	47
-60 to -65	17.8	45
-66 to -71	8.6	35
-72 to -77	3.2	31
-78 to -83	10.3	29
-84 to -138	9.1	110
Total	19.9	947

Note: Chi-square = 73.7, $p < .0001$; contingency coefficient = .27.

THE STRENGTH OF THE RELATIONSHIPS
BETWEEN THE INDEXES AND BEHAVIOR

When compared with the findings of most social science research in general and studies on drug behavior in particular, analyzed in comparable ways, the relationships shown in Tables 5.3 and
5.7 are relatively strong. Perhaps the strongest relationship between marijuana use and any other variable was reported by Kandel
(1973). She compared her young subjects who believed none of their
friends had used marijuana with those who believed all their friends
had used marijuana with respect to their own marijuana use, and
found that 7 percent of the former and 92 percent of the latter had
used marijuana. If an analogous comparison is made between the
extreme categories of the attribute-subjective probability index
(Table 5.7), the conclusion is that 9 percent of the subjects with the
most negative scores and 56 percent with the most positive scores
used marijuana one year later. For reasons discussed in Chapter 7,
weaker correlations are expected in panel studies such as the one
described in this book than in cross-sectional studies like Kandel's
due to inherent differences between these designs. In any case,
Kandel's findings are commonly used to highlight the importance of
peer use for the use of marijuana by others. Moreover, it is the
strongest relationship with marijuana use when one independent
variable is considered, and the relationships presented in this chapter approach this finding and appear stronger than most reported in
the balance of research on marijuana behavior.

OTHER ANALYSES

Several other analyses were conducted which are not presented
in detail here. First, there was some concern about the accuracy of
the classification of consequences as delayed or immediate. Clearly, it would have been desirable to have time during data collection
to allow the subjects to make these classifications. To determine
whether classification influenced the results presented, all analyses
reported in this chapter were repeated with several groupings of immediate and delayed consequences that differ from those shown in
Table 5.1. The findings with these different groups were virtually
identical to those reported. Second, most of the analyses in this
chapter were repeated, assigning a variety of time orientation scores.
For example, the sample was partitioned according to five categories
that ranged from 5 to 1 rather than 16 to 4 and then these measures
of time orientation were entered into the indexes. The results when
using these different scores for time orientation were virtually
identical to those shown.

CONCLUSION

There is a statistically significant and relatively strong relationship, in the hypothesized direction, between the utility structure index and subsequent behavior with marijuana. The attribute-subjective probability index explains variance in behavior beyond that accounted for by the attribute index alone, and the other indexes do not add to explained variance in marijuana use.

REFERENCE

Kandel, Denise. "Adolescent Marijuana Use: Role of Parents and Peers." Science 181 (1973): 1067-70.

6
RECENCY AND FREQUENCY OF
MARIJUANA USE

INTRODUCTION

One guiding hypothesis of the analyses presented in this chapter is that marijuana is used more recently and frequently by those with relatively positive utility structures. In this analysis were included the 131 subjects who indicated on their Round 1 questionnaires that they had used marijuana, and their Round 1 utility structures were related to the recency and frequency of use of marijuana as indicated on their Round 2 questionnaires. Relating Round 1 utility measures to Round 2 behavior is an attempt to determine whether the utility structure predicts subsequent behavior.

The indexes used to measure the utility structure and its components in this chapter are identical to those described in Chapter 5, and the derivation process is not repeated here. The distribution of the 131 Round 1 users on the time orientation scale, which is used in the utility structure index, is shown in Table 6.1. The recency of marijuana use was measured by the question, "How long has it been since you last used marijuana?" The response categories for that item and the distribution of subjects are shown in Table 6.2. The frequency of use of marijuana was measured by the question, "How many days have you used marijuana during the past 30 days?" The distribution on that variable is shown in Table 6.3. These two dependent variables are related ($r = .75$, $p < .0001$, $N = 131$), but they are considered separately in the analyses because the results vary somewhat by these two variables.

In addition to presenting the analysis to determine the relationship between Round 1 utility measures and Round 2 behavior, the relative contributions of the components of the utility structure to behavior are examined. The rationale for these analyses and the analysis strategies are analogous to those in the preceding chapter.

TABLE 6.1

Distribution on Time Orientation Scale as Measured in Round 1
(Sample: Users, Round 1)

Time Orientation	Number of Cases
16 (most present-oriented)	2
14	2
13	5
12	7
11	2
10	10
9	11
8	18
7	21
6	23
5	16
4 (most future-oriented)	14
Total	131

TABLE 6.2

Distribution on Recency of Use as Measured in Round 2
(Sample: Users, Round 1)

Recency of Use	Number of Cases
Today	18
1-7 days ago	48
8-14 days ago	20
15-30 days ago	15
31-90 days ago	8
91-180 days ago	6
181-365 days ago	6
>365 days ago	10
Total	131

TABLE 6.3

Distribution on Frequency of Use as Measured in Round 2
(Sample: Users, Round 1)

Number of Days Used During Last 30 Days	Number of Cases
>11	28
8–11	17
4–7	20
2–3	23
1	13
None	30
Total	131

RELATIONSHIP BETWEEN UTILITY STRUCTURE AND RECENCY AND FREQUENCY OF USE

The product-moment correlation between the utility structure index as measured in Round 1 and recency of use as measured in Round 2 for the 131 Round 1 users is .36, which is statistically significant ($p < .001$). It is also in the hypothesized direction; that is, the more positive the utility structure, the more recent the use of marijuana. The Round 1 utility structure index was also related to frequency of use in Round 2 in the direction of increased frequency with a more positive utility structure ($r = .34$, $p < .001$, $N = 131$). The hypothesis is confirmed.

Although the Round 1 utility structure predicts recency and frequency of use one year later, it is necessary to determine whether Round 1 recency and frequency account for these relationships. Since the Round 1 utility structure is correlated with Round 1 recency of use ($r = .37$, $p < .001$) and frequency of use ($r = .36$, $p < .001$), and there are relationships between the Round 1 and Round 2 measures of behavior ($r = .28$, $p < .001$ for recency, and $r = .33$, $p < .001$ for frequency), these relationships could account for the relationship between the Round 1 utility structure and Round 2 behavior. Perhaps Round 1 behavior rather than the Round 1 utility structure explains Round 2 behavior, possibly through the influence of behavior before Round 1 upon the Round 1 utility structure. Thus, Round 2 behavior might not be a consequence of the Round 1 utility structure even though they are associated. However, this is not the case; when controlling for Round 1 behavior by partial correlation, the relationship between Round 1 utility structure and Round 2 behavior remains statistically significant: $r = .33$, $p < .001$ when considering recency, and $r = .28$, $p < .001$ when considering frequency. Thus, the relationships between Round 1 utility structure and recency and frequency of use as measured in Round 2 are not accounted for by Round 1 behavior, and therefore it appears the relationships are not completely attributable to the influence of prior behavior upon the utility structure.

CONTRIBUTIONS OF THE COMPONENTS

Are all the components necessary for explaining the recency and frequency of marijuana use? The same component measures are used as those described in Chapter 5, and the same analysis strategy: six regression analyses with all combinations of the indexes entered, and those with the fewest components entered first. The results when considering the Round 1 indexes and Round 2 recency of use are shown in Table 6.4. The findings are clear: the attribute index is significant ($\underline{F} = 15.2$, $p < .01$) and only the time component adds a statistically significant amount of explained variance. Table 6.5 shows the results with Round 2 frequency of use as the dependent variable. In this case the attribute index is statistically significant ($\underline{F} = 13.5$, $p < .01$) but the addition of other components does not increase the amount of explained variance in use. The conclusion is that the attribute-time index and the attribute index predict recency and frequency of use, respectively, and that the other components make no additional contributions to the explanation of behavior.

This does not mean that the indexes representing other components are unrelated to behavior. Indeed, each index is related to behavior, as shown in Table 6.6, where the partials for Round 1 behavior are also shown. This relationship of each index with behavior is not surprising, given the strong correlations among indexes (Table 6.7). However, the addition of the other components is unnecessary because they do not increase the explanation of behavior by statistically significant amounts.

STRENGTH OF THE RELATIONSHIPS

The relationships between the indexes and recency or frequency of subsequent behavior, though statistically significant and

TABLE 6.4

Regression Analyses of Selected Combinations of Components as Measured
in Round 1 with Order of Entry Predetermined

(Sample: Users, Round 1; Dependent Variable: Recency of Use, Round 2; N = 131)

Analysis Number

1		2		3		4		5		6	
Order of entry:	F	Order of entry:	F	Order of entry:	F	Order of entry:	F	Order of entry:	F	Order of entry:	F
Attribute	15.2[a]	Attribute	15.2[a]	Attribute	15.2[a]	Attribute	15.2[a]	Attribute	15.2[a]	Attribute	15.2[a]
Attribute-salience	2.7	Attribute-salience	2.7	Attribute-subjective probability	1.7	Attribute-subjective probability	1.7	Attribute-time	6.5[b]	Attribute-time	6.5[b]
Attribute-salience-subjective probability	.8	Attribute-salience-time	5.4[b]	Attribute-subjective probability-salience	1.4	Attribute-subjective probability-time	5.4[b]	Attribute-time-salience	1.8	Attribute-time-subjective probability	.9
Attribute-salience-subjective probability-time	4.7[b]	Attribute-salience-subjective probability-time	.7	Attribute-salience-subjective probability-time	5.1[b]	Attribute-salience-subjective probability-time	1.3	Attribute-salience-subjective probability-time	.7	Attribute-salience-subjective probability-time	1.5

[a] $p < .01$ by $\underline{F}$ test.
[b] $p < .05$ by $\underline{F}$ test.

TABLE 6.5

Regression Analyses of Selected Combinations of Components as Measured
in Round 1 with Order of Entry Predetermined

(Sample: Users, Round 1; Dependent Variable: Frequency of Use, Round 2; N = 131)

Analysis Number

	1		2		3		4		5		6	
	Order of entry:	F	Order of entry:	F	Order of entry:	F	Order of entry:	F	Order of entry:	F	Order of entry:	F
	Attribute	13.5*	Attribute	13.5*	Attribute	13.5*	Attribute	13.5*	Attribute	13.5*	Attribute	13.5*
	Attribute-salience	2.1	Attribute-salience	2.1	Attribute-subjective probability	2.0	Attribute-subjective probability	2.0	Attribute-time	3.3	Attribute-time	3.3
	Attribute-salience-subjective probability	.8	Attribute-salience-time	3.0	Attribute-subjective probability-salience	.7	Attribute-subjective probability-time	2.8	Attribute-time-salience	1.7	Attribute-time-subjective probability	1.4
	Attribute-salience-subjective probability-time	2.7	Attribute-salience-subjective probability-time	.7	Attribute-salience-subjective probability-time	3.0	Attribute-salience-subjective probability-time	.9	Attribute-salience-subjective probability-time	.8	Attribute-salience-subjective probability-time	.9

*p < .01 by F test.

TABLE 6.6

Correlations between Round 1 Indexes and Round 2 Recency and Frequency of Use, and Partial Correlations Controlling for Round 1 Recency and Frequency
(N = 131)

Round 1 Index	Round 1 Index by Round 2 Recency	Round 1 Index by Round 2 Recency, Partial for Round 1 Recency	Round 1 Index by Round 2 Frequency	Round 1 Index by Round 2 Frequency, Partial for Round 1 Frequency
Attribute	.32	.25	.31	.22
Attribute–salience	.35	.27	.33	.23
Attribute–subjective probability	.34	.28	.33	.25
Attribute–time	.39	.33	.34	.25
Attribute–salience–subjective probability	.36	.28	.34	.25
Attribute–salience–time	.40	.33	.36	.26
Attribute–subjective probability–time	.39	.34	.36	.28
Attribute–salience–subjective probability–time	.40	.33	.36	.28

Note: Each correlation (product-moment) has $p < .01$.

69

TABLE 6.7

Correlation Matrix of Combinations of Components as Measured in Round 1
(Sample: Users, Round 1; N = 131)

	Attribute	Attribute-Salience	Attribute-Subjective Probability	Attribute-Time	Attribute-Salience-Subjective Probability	Attribute-Salience-Time	Attribute-Subjective Probability-Time	Attribute-Salience-Subjective Probability-Time
Attribute	1.00	—						
Attribute-salience	.95	1.00	—					
Attribute-subjective probability	.92	.88	1.00					
Attribute-time	.85	.82	.81	1.00	—	—	—	—
Attribute-salience-subjective probability	.89	.94	.96	.78	1.00	—	—	—
Attribute-salience-time	.84	.90	.79	.94	.83	1.00	—	—
Attribute-subjective probability-time	.81	.79	.88	.95	.84	.90	1.00	—
Attribute-salience-subjective probability-time	.82	.87	.86	.91	.90	.95	.95	1.00

Note: All correlations statistically significant at $p < .001$ (Pearson r).

in the hypothesized directions, do not appear by themselves to be very strong: they are all below .40 in Table 6.6, and therefore none of the indexes explains more than 16 percent of the variation in recency and frequency one year later. However, the strength of these correlations compares quite favorably with those from other research designed to identify predictors of marijuana behavior (see, for example, the studies summarized and referenced in Jessor 1979, Lettieri 1975, and Kandel 1978), and in this sense could be considered important. Further consideration is given in Chapter 7 to the importance of these relationships, using different criteria for assessing importance.

CONCLUSION

Both recency and frequency of marijuana use are related in the hypothesized direction to the indexes measured one year earlier. These relationships persist when adjusted for Round 1 behavior, but appear modest in strength when considered by themselves. When compared with correlations found in other studies the size of the correlations fare quite well. When considering recency of use, the attribute-time index is the index with the fewest components that adds a significant amount of explained variance in behavior beyond that accounted for by the attribute index. For frequency of use, addition of components beyond the attribute do not add a statistically significant amount of explained variance in behavior.

REFERENCES

Jessor, Richard. "Marijuana: A Review of Recent Psychosocial Research." In Handbook on Drug Abuse, edited by Robert I. Dupont, Avram Goldstein, and John O'Donnel, pp. 337-55. Washington, D.C.: Government Printing Office, 1979.

Kandel, Denise, ed. Longitudinal Research on Drug Use: Empirical Findings and Methodological Issues. New York: Wiley, 1978.

Lettieri, Dan J., ed. Predicting Adolescent Drug Abuse: A Review of Issues, Methods and Correlates, DHEW Publication No. (ADM) 76-299. Washington, D.C.: Government Printing Office, 1975.

7

A COMPARISON OF THE UTILITY
STRUCTURE AND ANTECEDENT VARIABLES
AS CORRELATES OF BEHAVIOR

The findings presented in Chapters 5 and 6 consistently revealed statistically significant relationships in the hypothesized
direction between the utility structure index (and other indexes) as
measured in Round 1 with marijuana behavior as reported on the
Round 2 questionnaires. It was concluded that the relationships
compared quite favorably in strength with those found in earlier research on drug behavior. In this chapter a different criterion is
used for considering the importance of the utility structure. At the
outset, it is recognized that the variables classified as antecedent
in the Chapter 1 discussion of the theoretical model have been considered by others as determinants of behavior with marijuana. The
antecedent variables measured in this study are listed in Table 7.1.
It is hypothesized that the utility structure may also be a determinant of behavior with marijuana. In this chapter the utility structure index and the antecedent variables are compared with respect
to their relative contributions to explaining variance in marijuana
behavior. If the utility structure index and other indexes compare
favorably with the antecedent variables as predictors of behavior,
then the utility structure will be considered a relatively important
variable for explaining behavior. If, on the other hand, the antecedent variables prove to be more powerful predictors of marijuana
behavior than the utility structure, then the utility structure will be
declared a relatively unimportant variable for explaining behavior
with marijuana.

Note that the consideration of the antecedent variables here
differs from what was suggested in the theoretical model. Specifically, as indicated in Chapter 1, the utility structure is considered as a
variable that might explain why the antecedent variables are related
to behavior with marijuana. Chapter 8 will present analyses designed to test that hypothesis. In this chapter the indexes are compared with the antecedent variables to assess their relative contributions to explaining variance in marijuana behavior.

TABLE 7.1

Hypothesized Relationships of Selected Antecedent Variables
with Behavior and the Utility Structure Index

Antecedent Variable*	Categories of Subjects for Whom Marijuana Use Is Relatively Likely (and Recent and Frequent), and the Utility Structure Index Is Relatively Positive
Perceived availability of marijuana	Those who perceive marijuana as easy to obtain
Drug education in school	Those who have not had drug education
Talk with friends about marijuana	Those who have talked with friends about marijuana
Friend's use of marijuana	Those who have friends who have used marijuana
Aspiration for college	Those who do not aspire to college
Likelihood of attending college	Those who believe their chances for college are low
Closeness to father	Those who do not feel close to their fathers
Closeness to mother	Those who do not feel close to their mothers
Sex	Males
Race	Whites
Age	Older students
Sociability	Sociable students
Friend-parent influence	Those who are influenced more by friends than by parents
Rebelliousness	Rebellious students
Boredom	Bored students
Curiosity	Curious individuals
Permissiveness of parents	Those who have permissive parents
Stress	Those who have stress
Religiosity	Those who are not religious

*Underlined words are used in text to indicate variable.

TABLE 7.2

Descriptive Information on Single-Item Antecedent Variables as Measured in Round 1, by Group

Question* Number	Antecedent Variable	Categories	Percent			
			Round 1 and 2 Nonusers (N = 683)	Round 1 Nonusers/ Round 2 Users (N = 163)	Round 1 Users (N = 103)	Total (N = 949)
3.	Availability	1. very hard	41.0	24.5	9.7	34.8
		2. somewhat hard	31.8	17.8	13.6	27.4
		3. somewhat easy	20.8	33.7	36.9	24.8
		4. very easy	6.4	23.9	39.8	13.1
4.	Drug education	1. yes	74.1	71.8	68.9	73.1
		2. no	25.9	28.2	31.1	26.9
5.	Talk with friends	1. never	37.5	22.1	2.9	31.1
		2. seldom	43.3	36.8	15.5	39.2
		3. sometimes	16.3	28.8	33.0	20.2
		4. often	2.9	12.3	48.5	9.5
6.	Friend's use	1. neither has used	69.4	47.2	11.7	59.3
		2. don't know	24.2	27.6	9.7	23.2
		3. one has used	5.7	21.5	33.0	11.4
		4. both have used	0.7	3.7	45.6	6.1
62.	Aspiration	1. very much	67.3	60.1	39.8	63.1
		2. somewhat	21.8	20.2	27.2	22.1
		3. not very much	7.5	14.7	19.4	10.0
		4. not at all	3.4	4.9	13.6	4.7

No.	Category					
63.	Likelihood of college	1. absolutely certain	32.7	19.0	17.5	28.7
		2. very likely	42.8	46.0	30.1	41.9
		3. somewhat likely	17.4	19.0	20.4	18.0
		4. not very likely	5.0	12.9	24.3	8.4
		5. impossible	2.2	3.1	7.8	3.0
64.	Closeness to father	1. extremely close	48.3	36.2	20.4	43.2
		2. quite close	29.1	36.2	32.0	30.7
		3. moderately close	14.8	12.9	25.2	15.6
		4. not particularly close	6.3	9.2	14.6	7.7
		5. not at all close	1.5	5.5	7.8	2.8
65	Closeness to mother	1. extremely close	59.6	56.4	35.0	56.4
		2. quite close	27.2	25.2	21.4	26.2
		3. moderately close	10.5	10.4	28.2	12.4
		4. not particularly close	2.3	6.1	10.7	3.9
		5. not at all close	0.3	1.8	4.9	1.1
81.	Sex	1. female	63.4	51.5	41.7	59.0
		2. male	36.6	48.5	58.3	41.0
82.	Race	1. nonwhite	11.3	12.9	10.7	11.5
		2. white	88.7	87.1	89.3	88.5
83.	Age	1. 10 or younger	0.0	0.0	1.0	0.1
		2. 11	0.4	0.0	0.0	0.3
		3. 12	42.9	34.4	21.4	39.1
		4. 13	53.3	59.5	61.2	55.2
		5. 14	3.4	4.9	11.7	4.5
		6. 15	0.0	1.2	2.9	0.5
		7. 16 or older	0.0	0.0	1.9	0.2

*From Section C of Questionnaire (Appendix A).

MEASUREMENT OF THE ANTECEDENT VARIABLES

Antecedent variables that had been found predictive of drug behavior in earlier research were selected for study. (See, for example, Jessor 1979, Lettieri 1975, and Kandel 1978). Most measures of these variables were adapted on the basis of pilot studies of those indexed in Nehemkis, Macari, and Lettieri (1976). These variables are listed in the first column of Table 7.1. Next to each variable in that table is summarized the hypothesis regarding the relationship of the antecedent variable and the utility structure with marijuana behavior. All these variables were coded for analysis in the direction of high score equal to use of marijuana (and frequency, and recency of use) and positive utility structure. Thus, all positive relationships shown in this chapter are in the hypothesized direction, and negative associations are opposite to the directions hypothesized.

In Table 7.2 descriptive information is provided on the single-item antecedent variables for the main subgroups of the sample. The number to the left of each variable name corresponds to the number of that item in the questionnaire (Appendix A). The codes used in analysis are shown next to the category of each item. Cases with missing information on one or more of these variables are omitted from all analyses in this chapter.

Table 7.3 provides descriptive information for the multiple-item antecedent variables. The items from the questionnaire (Appendix A) used to measure these variables are shown to the left of each variable. The summary scores for the multiple-item variables were derived by summing the values for items. In the few cases missing one or more items on a variable, but answering at least one item for that variable, the missing items were assigned the average of all items that had been answered before summing all items for the variable. Subjects who missed all items for any multiple-item variable were eliminated from all analyses in this chapter.

The educational levels of students' mothers and fathers were measured, but omitted as antecedent variables because many students did not know their parents' educational levels. After deleting those items there were 129 subjects who gave insufficient information on their questionnaires to classify them according to one or more of the other antecedent variables. That is, these cases had missing information for one or more of the single-item variables, or missing information for all items of one or more multiple-item variables. These cases were omitted from all analyses in this chapter, yielding 949 subjects. Of these 949, 683 indicated on both their Round 1 and Round 2 questionnaires they had never used

TABLE 7.3

Descriptive Information on Multiple-item Antecedent Variables as Measured in Round 1, by Group

Question* Number	Antecedent Variable	Round 1 and 2 Nonusers (N = 683)				Round 1 Nonusers/Round 2 Users (N = 163)			
		Mean	Standard Deviation	Range Actual	Range Possible	Mean	Standard Deviation	Range Actual	Range Possible
39–47	Sociability	28.1	6.9	9.0–50.0	9.0–54.0	31.4	7.6	9.0–46.0	9.0–54.0
48–49	Friend-parent influence	5.4	1.9	2.0–10.0	2.0–10.0	6.3	1.9	2.0–10.0	2.0–10.0
50–53	Rebelliousness	5.0	1.0	4.0– 8.0	4.0– 8.0	5.6	1.1	4.0– 8.0	4.0– 8.0
54–58	Boredom	9.7	2.5	5.0–20.0	5.0–20.0	10.0	2.8	5.0–19.0	5.0–20.0
59–61	Curiosity	7.6	1.5	3.0–12.0	3.0–12.0	8.2	1.5	4.0–12.0	3.0–12.0
66–71	Permissiveness	9.5	1.4	6.0–12.0	6.0–12.0	10.0	1.3	7.0–12.0	6.0–12.0
72–78	Stress	12.3	2.8	7.0–21.0	7.0–21.0	12.6	2.8	7.0–20.0	7.0–21.0
79–80	Religiosity	3.5	1.6	2.0– 8.0	2.0– 8.0	4.3	1.9	2.0– 8.0	2.0– 8.0

Question* Number	Antecedent Variable	Round 1 Users (N = 103)				Total (N = 949)			
		Mean	Standard Deviation	Range Actual	Range Possible	Mean	Standard Deviation	Range Actual	Range Possible
39–47	Sociability	35.6	7.0	21.0–51.0	9.0–54.0	29.5	7.5	9.0–51.0	9.0–54.0
48–49	Friend-parent influence	7.3	2.1	4.0–10.0	2.0–10.0	5.7	2.0	2.0–10.0	2.0–10.0
50–53	Rebelliousness	6.1	1.2	4.0– 8.0	4.0– 8.0	5.2	1.1	4.0– 8.0	4.0– 8.0
54–58	Boredom	10.2	2.6	5.0–17.0	5.0–20.0	9.8	2.6	5.0–20.0	5.0–20.0
59–61	Curiosity	8.5	2.0	3.0–12.0	3.0–12.0	7.8	1.6	3.0–12.0	3.0–12.0
66–71	Permissiveness	10.0	1.3	7.0–12.0	6.0–12.0	9.6	1.4	6.0–12.0	6.0–12.0
72–78	Stress	13.1	3.0	7.0–21.0	7.0–21.0	12.4	2.8	7.0–21.0	7.0–21.0
79–80	Religiosity	4.7	1.6	2.0– 8.0	2.0– 8.0	3.8	1.7	2.0– 8.0	2.0– 8.0

*Section C of Questionnaire (Appendix A).

marijuana, 163 indicated they had not used marijuana by Round 1 but had by Round 2, and 103 said on both questionnaires that they had used marijuana.

Omitting the 129 subjects with missing information on the antecedent variables did not eliminate the relationship between the utility structure and behavior observed in Chapters 5 and 6, as can be seen by inspecting any table presented in this chapter.

ANALYSIS STRATEGY

The analysis strategy was to enter 20 independent variables—the 19 antecedent variables and the utility structure index—in a stepwise regression with marijuana behavior as the dependent variable. The index and antecedent variables were measured in Round 1, and the behavior measure is from the Round 2 questionnaire. If the utility structure index enters early it is considered a relatively important variable, whereas if it does not enter or enters after many of the antecedent variables, it is concluded that relative to the antecedent variables the index is unimportant. Analyses were also conducted using the indexes with the smaller number of components, as identified through analyses presented in Chapters 5 and 6. When considering Round 1 nonusers, the dependent variable is whether marijuana was used by Round 2, and when considering Round 1 users, the dependent variable is either Round 2 recency or frequency of use.

Results for Round 1 Nonusers

The data for those who said on their Round 1 questionnaire that they had never used marijuana are presented first. Round 2 use of marijuana is the dependent variable. Table 7.4 summarizes the results of the stepwise regression in which the 20 independent variables were allowed to enter in order of the greatest amount of variance explained in behavior. The eight variables listed in the left column of Table 7.4 explain statistically significant amounts of variance in Round 2 behavior, and the 12 variables not shown in the table do not explain additional variance in behavior that is statistically significant. Of the eight variables that did enter, the utility structure index enters fifth, and is preceded by availability, friend's use, sociability, and religiosity. Thus, by the criterion used here those four variables are more important predictors of behavior than the utility structure index. However, 15 antecedent variables—the three that entered after the index and the 12 that did not enter—are less important predictors of behavior than the index.

TABLE 7.4

Stepwise Regression of the Utility Structure Index and
Antecedent Variables as Measured for Round 1 on
Use as Measured for Round 2
(Sample: Nonusers, Round 1; N = 846)

Independent Variables	Beta	B	Standard Error	R^2	F	p
Availability	.126	.050	.014	.064	13.47	.0003
Friend's use	.144	.080	.018	.101	18.90	.0001
Sociability	.135	.007	.002	.139	17.52	.0001
Religiosity	.108	.025	.008	.154	10.73	.0011
Utility structure index	.090	.00004	.00002	.163	7.27	.0071
Talk with friends	.090	.042	.016	.170	6.89	.0088
Likelihood of college	.073	.029	.013	.175	4.97	.0260
Friend-parent influence	.075	.016	.007	.178	5.07	.0246
Intercept	—	.498	—	—	—	—

Term	df	Mean Square	F	p
Regression	8	2.883	22.23	.0001
Error	837	.130		

Table 7.5 shows these analyses repeated with the attribute-subjective probability index substituted for the utility structure index. Eight variables entered and 12 did not. The index entered third. It was concluded that the attribute-subjective probability index explains more variance in marijuana use than most of the 19 antecedent variables, but less variance than availability and friend's use.

Results for Round 1 Users

Next, the data are analyzed for those subjects who reported during Round 1 that they had used marijuana, and recency of use as measured in Round 2 is considered the dependent variable. The results when entering the utility structure index and the 19 antecedent variables are summarized in Table 7.6. The utility structure index entered first, and three of the antecedent variables entered next. Sixteen of the antecedent variables did not enter, and therefore did not explain a statistically significant amount of variance in behavior beyond that already accounted for by the four that did enter. This analysis is repeated when the attribute-time index is substituted for the utility structure index (Table 7.7) and a similar conclusion is derived: The index entered first, followed by two antecedent variables, and the remaining 17 variables did not add to the explanation of variance in recency beyond that attributable to the three that entered.

TABLE 7.5

Stepwise Regression of the Attribute-Subjective Probability
Index and Antecedent Variables as Measured for Round 1
on Use as Measured for Round 2
(Sample: Nonusers, Round 1; N = 846)

Independent Variables	Beta	B	Standard Error	R^2	F	p
Availability	.124	.049	.014	.064	13.11	.0003
Friend's use	.145	.081	.018	.101	19.33	.0001
Attribute-subjective probability index	.102	.0013	.0004	.125	9.32	.0023
Sociability	.133	.007	.0018	.145	17.21	.0001
Religiosity	.104	.024	.008	.159	9.95	.0017
Talk with friends	.087	.041	.016	.168	6.51	.0109
Likelihood of college	.070	.028	.0132	.177	4.57	.0328
Intercept	—	.508	—	—	—	—

Term	df	Mean Square	F	p
Regression	8	2.92	22.54	.0001
Error	837	.129		

TABLE 7.6

Stepwise Regression of the Utility Structure Index and Antecedent
Variables as Measured for Round 1 on Recency of Use as
Measured for Round 2 (Sample: Users, Round 1; N = 103)

Independent Variables	Beta	B	Standard Error	R^2	F	p
Utility structure index	.400	.001	.0002	.148	19.53	.0001
Permissiveness	.298	.460	.132	.212	12.06	.0008
Race	-.216	-1.413	.590	.265	5.72	.0187
Aspiration	.187	.355	.165	.298	4.60	.0344
Intercept	—	3.354	—	—	—	—

Term	df	Mean Square	F	p
Regression	4	31.380	10.39	.0001
Error	98	3.020		

TABLE 7.7

Stepwise Regression of the Attribute-Time Index and Antecedent
Variables as Measured for Round 1 on Recency of Use as
Measured for Round 2 (Sample: Users, Round 1; N = 103)

Independent Variables	Beta	B	Standard Error	R^2	F	p
Attribute-time index	.335	.017	.005	.143	14.72	.0002
Permissiveness	.284	.438	.134	.211	10.61	.0015
Aspiration	.224	.426	.167	.260	6.52	.0122
Intercept	—	.786	—	—	—	—

Term	df	Mean Square	F	p
Regression	3	36.507	11.59	.0001
Error	99	3.150		

The conclusions when considering frequency of use as the dependent variable are the same as when using recency of use. Three variables entered when considering the utility structure index and the antecedent variables, with the utility structure index entering first (Table 7. 8). Thus, by using order of entry as a criterion for importance, the index is a more important correlate of behavior than any of the 19 antecedent variables. When substituting the attribute index for the utility structure index in a regression on frequency (Table 7. 9), three variables entered, with the index entering first.

AMOUNT OF VARIANCE

Viewing the values of R^2 generated by these analyses and presented in the tables indicates the portion of variance in the dependent variable that is explained by the independent variables that enter the regression. When considering Round 1 nonusers, the amount of variance in Round 2 use accounted for by all independent variables that entered was 17. 8 percent (R^2 = .178) with the utility structure index and 25. 5 percent (R^2 = .255) with the attribute-subjective probability index. The total variance explained when considering recency or frequency of use as dependent variables ranged from 19. 3 percent (Table 7. 9) to 29. 8 percent (Table 7. 6). Obviously, most of the variance in marijuana behavior remains to be explained. In the regressions for which an index entered first, the amount of variance explained by the index ranged from 8. 4 percent (Table 7. 9) to 18. 0 percent (Table 7. 5). It is clear that only a small portion of the variance in behavior is accounted for by the indexes.

In general the R^2 values compare quite favorably with those found in other research implemented to identify predictors of marijuana behavior. (See, for example, the studies summarized and cited in Jessor 1979, Kandel 1978, and Lettieri 1975.) However, it is necessary to qualify any comparison of an R^2 from this study with those found in other research. One reason for this is that they are not directly comparable as a result of the varying analysis strategies used in the studies. Another reason is that much of the earlier research on marijuana behavior used cross-sectional rather than panel designs. Since cross-sectional designs deal with the measures taken at one point in time, and because these designs typically do not control for reciprocal relationships, it is suspected that cross-sectional studies have a greater chance for explaining variance in behavior than panel designs. However, the amount of variance explained in this research also compares favorably with earlier panel studies of drug behavior (Kandel 1978). Given this perspective, the amount

TABLE 7.8

Stepwise Regression of the Utility Structure Index and Antecedent Variables as Measured for Round 1 on Frequency of Use as Measured for Round 2 (Sample: Users, Round 1; N = 103)

Independent Variables	Beta	$\underline{B}$	Standard Error	$\underline{R}^2$	$\underline{F}$	$\underline{p}$
Utility structure index	.302	.0007	.0002	.123	11.02	.0013
Aspiration	.227	.393	.158	.164	6.21	.0144
Permissiveness	.201	.283	.127	.204	4.96	.0282
Intercept	—	-.035	—	—	—	—

Term	$\underline{df}$	Mean Square	$\underline{F}$	$\underline{p}$
Regression	3	23.753	8.46	.0001
Error	99	2.808		

TABLE 7.9

Stepwise Regression of the Attribute Index and Antecedent Variables as Measured for Round 1 on Frequency of Use as Measured for Round 2 (Sample: Users, Round 1; N = 103)

Independent Variables	Beta	$\underline{B}$	Standard Error	$\underline{R}^2$	$\underline{F}$	$\underline{p}$
Attribute index	.279	.088	.028	.084	9.52	.0026
Aspiration	.268	.464	.157	.145	8.74	.0039
Permissiveness	.220	.309	.128	.193	5.88	.0172
Intercept	—	-.573	—	—	—	—

Term	$\underline{df}$	Mean Square	$\underline{F}$	$\underline{p}$
Regression	3	22.471	7.89	.0001
Error	99	2.846		

of variance explained in this present study appears quite good when compared with most earlier research.

CONCLUSION

Using the criterion that variables entering early in regression analyses are more important correlates of behavior than those that enter later or never enter, it was found that the index always entered early and sometimes entered first when considered along with 19 other variables often considered determinants of behavior with marijuana. The amount of variance explained by these regression models is not substantial—specifically, most of the variance remained unexplained for the study samples—but it compares favorably with other studies of marijuana behavior.

REFERENCES

Jessor, Richard. "Marijuana: A Review of Recent Psychosocial Research." In Handbook on Drug Abuse, edited by Robert I. Dupont, Avram Goldstein, and John O'Donnel, pp. 337-55. Washington, D.C.: Government Printing Office, 1979.

Kandel, Denise, ed. Longitudinal Research on Drug Use: Empirical Findings and Methodological Issues. New York: Wiley, 1978.

Lettieri, Dan J., ed. Predicting Adolescent Drug Abuse: A Review of Issues, Methods and Correlates, DHEW Publication No. (ADM) 76-299. Washington, D.C.: Government Printing Office, 1975.

Nehemkis, Alexis, Mary A. Macari, and Dan J. Lettieri, eds. Drug Abuse Instrument Handbook (Research Issues 12), DHEW Publication No. (ADM) 76-394. Washington, D.C.: Government Printing Office, 1976.

8
ANTECEDENT VARIABLES, THE UTILITY STRUCTURE, AND BEHAVIOR

INTRODUCTION

Many variables that have been considered determinants of behavior with marijuana are not readily classifiable as attributes. These are called antecedent in the theoretical framework, and a selected list of them was presented in the first column of Table 7.1. The research was begun with the general hypothesis that if these antecedent variables influence behavior with marijuana, they do so by affecting the utility structure, which in turn influences behavior with marijuana. Examples of this reasoning were given in Chapter 1 when considering several antecedent variables, and it is examined as a hypothesis in this chapter. One necessary link in this chain of reasoning exists for the data—the positive relationship between the utility structure and behavior with marijuana—as has already been demonstrated in Chapters 5, 6, and 7.

If the utility structure explains the relationship between an antecedent variable and behavior with marijuana, then the relationship between the antecedent variable and the utility structure, and the relationship between the antecedent variable and marijuana behavior, should be statistically significant and in consistent directions. For example, given the observed positive relationship between the utility structure and subsequent behavior with marijuana, if subjects whose peers use marijuana are more likely to use marijuana than subjects whose peers do not use marijuana, and peer use is positively related to the utility structure, then these relationships are compatible with the hypothesis that peer use influences behavior with marijuana through its impact on the utility structure. If either or both of these relationships do not exist, or relationships are present but in inconsistent directions—for example, subjects whose peers use marijuana are more likely to use marijuana than subjects whose peers do not use marijuana, but peer use and the utility structure are _inversely_ related—then the hypothesis that the utility explains why the antecedent variable and behavior with marijuana are related would be untenable.

Even when relationships exist among an antecedent variable, the utility structure, and behavior, and these are in hypothesized directions, the utility structure may not explain the relationship between the antecedent variable and behavior. Thus, when these relationships are present and in hypothesized directions, it is necessary to control for the utility structure to determine if it accounts for the relationship between the antecedent variable and behavior. These analyses are presented in this chapter.

All analyses that include the utility structure index are repeated with the index having the reduced combination of components identified through the components analyses presented in Chapters 5 and 6. The measures of antecedent variables, and the subjects included in these analyses, are identical to those described in the preceding chapter.

ROUND 1 NONUSERS

Those subjects who said on the Round 1 questionnaire that they had never used marijuana are considered first, using the measure of their Round 1 utility structure, Round 1 antecedent variables, and their use or nonuse of marijuana by Round 2. Regression analyses are used to first identify antecedent variables that are related to both the utility structure index and behavior with marijuana, and in directions consistent with the hypothesis that the utility structure intervenes between the antecedent variable and behavior. Then, by another application of regression analysis, the relationships between these antecedent variables and behavior are viewed, first allowing the utility structure index to explain as much variance in behavior as it can. By using this analysis strategy it is possible to test the hypothesis that the antecedent variable influences behavior through its effect on the utility structure. If there are no relationships between these antecedent variables and behavior when controlling for the utility structure, it is concluded that the utility structure explains the relationship; whereas if the relationships persist between antecedent variables and behavior after controlling for the index, it is concluded that the index does not explain all the association between the antecedent variables and behavior. Since the attribute-subjective probability index explained maximum variance in behavior with the fewest components, these analyses are repeated when that index is substituted for the utility structure index.

Table 8.1 summarizes the results of the regression of the antecedent variables upon the use of marijuana. Eight of the 19 antecedent variables had statistically significant relationships with Round 2 use of marijuana, and all relationships were in the hypothesized direction. Those eight variables are listed in the left hand column of Table 8.1. Antecedent variables that are not shown in Table 8.1 were not related to behavior in this model. Table 8.2 shows the results of the regression of all antecedent variables on the utility structure index. Eight of the 19 antecedent variables had statistically significant relationships with the Round 1 utility structure index, and with the exception of stress, these were related in the hypothesized direction. The 11 antecedent variables not listed in Table 8.2 were not related to the utility structure index in this model. A comparison of Tables 8.1 and 8.2 reveals that four antecedent variables are related in directions consistent with the hypothesis that the utility structure explains their relationship with use of marijuana: friend's use, rebelliousness, friend-parent influence, and likelihood of college. Table 8.3 shows the results of the regression analysis in which the utility structure index is forced to enter as the first independent variable, and the four antecedent variables with common links to the utility structure and behavior are allowed to enter next. The antecedent variables still explain statistically significant amounts of variance in use under this condition, and therefore it is concluded that the utility structure does not account for their relationship with behavior.

These analyses were repeated with the attribute-subjective probability index substituted for the utility structure index. Table 8.4 lists the nine antecedent variables that are related to the attribute-subjective probability index. The ten antecedent variables not shown in Table 8.4 are unrelated to the index in this model. Five of the antecedent variables that are related to the attribute-subjective probability index also have positive and significant associations with marijuana use, as can be seen by comparing Tables 8.4 and 8.1. Table 8.5 summarizes the regression analysis in which the attribute-subjective probability index is forced to enter first, with these five antecedent variables entered next. In this model each of the antecedent variables adds a statistically significant amount of explained variance with the exception of likelihood of college. Thus, the attribute-subjective probability index accounts for the relationship between likelihood of college and use of marijuana, but the index does not account for the relationships between the other four antecedent variables and behavior.

TABLE 8.1

Stepwise Regression of the 19 Antecedent Variables as Measured for Round 1 on Use as Measured for Round 2 (Sample: Nonusers, Round 1; N = 846)

Independent Variables	Beta	B	Standard Error	R^2	F	p
Availability	.127	.050	.014	.064	13.67	.0002
Friend's use	.140	.078	.019	.101	17.59	.0001
Rebelliousness	.078	.030	.014	.124	4.91	.0269
Sociability	.124	.007	.002	.139	14.53	.0001
Religiosity	.107	.025	.008	.154	10.38	.0013
Talk with friends	.084	.039	.016	.162	5.99	.0146
Friend-parent influence	.078	.016	.007	.168	5.41	.0203
Likelihood of college	.074	.030	.013	.173	5.18	.0231
Intercept	—	.306	—	—	—	—

Term	df	Mean Square	F	p
Regression	8	2.845	21.88	.0001
Error	837	.130		

TABLE 8.2

Stepwise Regression of the 19 Antecedent Variables as Measured for Round 1 on the Utility Structure Index as Measured for Round 1 (Sample: Nonusers, Round 1; N = 846)

Independent Variables	Beta	B	Standard Error	R^2	F	p
Rebelliousness	.183	152.791	29.194	.079	27.39	.0001
Friend-parent influence	.130	58.577	15.531	.106	14.23	.0002
Likelihood of college	.098	85.835	29.410	.121	8.52	.0036
Closeness to father	.071	58.434	27.940	.128	4.37	.0368
Permissiveness	.079	46.810	19.512	.135	5.76	.0167
Friend's use	.080	96.310	39.984	.140	5.80	.0162
Boredom	.099	32.892	11.840	.145	7.72	.0056
Stress	-.086	-26.526	10.529	.152	6.35	.0119
Intercept	—	-3381.659	—	—	—	—

Term	df	Mean Square	F	p
Regression	8	11738113.627	18.73	.0001
Error	837	626858.891		

TABLE 8.3

Regression on Use as Measured for Round 2 with the Utility Structure
Index as Measured for Round 1 Entered First and Four Selected
Antecedent Variables as Measured for Round 1 Entered Next
(Sample: Nonusers, Round 1; N = 846)

Independent Variables	Beta	B	Standard Error	R^2	F	p
Utility structure index	.096	.0000443	.00002	.040	7.73	<.01
Friend's use	.175	.0976	.019	.086	27.25	<.01
Rebelliousness	.127	.0492	.014	.108	12.92	<.01
Friend-parent influence	.113	.0235	.007	.120	11.05	<.01
Likelihood of college	.068	.0278	.013	.125	4.25	<.05
Intercept	—	.671	—	—	—	—

Term	df	Mean Square	F	p
Regression	5	3.284	23.95	<.01
Error	840	.137		

TABLE 8.4

Stepwise Regression of the 19 Antecedent Variables as Measured for
Round 1 on the Attribute-Subjective Probability Index as
Measured for Round 1
(Sample: Nonusers, Round 1; N = 846)

Independent Variables	Beta	B	Standard Error	R^2	F	p
Rebelliousness	.171	5.238	1.069	.093	23.99	.0001
Friend-parent influence	.109	1.802	.573	.117	9.90	.0017
Likelihood of college	.092	2.962	1.073	.135	7.61	.0059
Permissiveness	.099	2.161	.707	.147	9.34	.0023
Boredom	.087	1.059	.417	.155	6.46	.0112
Availability	.077	2.429	1.026	.162	5.61	.0181
Sex	.079	5.077	2.116	.168	5.76	.0166
Closeness to father	.068	2.071	1.019	.172	4.13	.0424
Religiosity	.066	1.213	.615	.176	3.89	.0488
Intercept	—	-138.121	—	—	—	—

Term	df	Mean Square	F	p
Regression	9	16289.0005	19.87	.0001
Error	836	819.686		

TABLE 8.5

Regression on Use as Measured for Round 2 with the
Attribute-Subjective Probability Index as Measured
for Round 1 Entered First and Five Selected
Antecedent Variables as Measured for
Round 1 Entered Next
(Sample: Nonusers, Round 1; N = 846)

Independent Variables	Beta	B	Standard Error	R^2	F	p
Attribute-subjective probability index	.107	.00135	.0004	.047	9.64	<.01
Availability	.179	.0704	.013	.095	28.65	<.01
Rebelliousness	.123	.0474	.014	.117	12.23	<.01
Religiosity	.110	.0256	.008	.130	10.86	<.01
Friend-parent influence	.087	.0180	.007	.137	6.41	<.05
Intercept	—	.670	—	—	—	—
Variable that does not enter Likelihood of college	.056	.0228	.014	.140	2.85	N.S.

Term	df	Mean Square	F	p
Regression	5	3.607	26.68	<.01
Error	840	.135		

ROUND 1 USERS

Analyses were conducted to determine whether the utility structure index explains the relationship between antecedent variables and the recency and frequency of marijuana use, considering the subjects who reported on their Round 1 questionnaire that they had used marijuana, the antecedent variables and utility structure index as measured for Round 1, and Round 2 recency and frequency of use of marijuana. First, the antecedent variables were identified that are statistically related in the hypothesized direction with both behavior and the utility structure index. Then in a regression on behavior, the utility structure index was entered first and these antecedent variables second. If the antecedent variables are not significantly related to behavior under this condition it is concluded that the utility structure index explains their relationship with behavior. If, on the other hand, these antecedent variables are related to behavior after the utility structure index has entered first, it is concluded that the index does not explain all the relationship between antecedent variables and behavior. All these analyses are done separately when considering recency and frequency of use, and repeated with the attribute-time index when considering recency and the attribute index when considering frequency.

Table 8.6 summarizes the regression between the antecedent variables and recency of use. Three variables are related in the hypothesized direction with recency of use: permissiveness, aspiration, and age. Table 8.7 shows the results of the regression of the antecedent variables on the utility structure index, with five variables that are related: friend's use, age, race, sociability, and sex. All are in the hypothesized direction except sex. Only age has a common association with the utility structure index and recency of use, as seen by comparing Tables 8.6 and 8.7. Table 8.8 shows the results of the regression on recency when the utility structure index is entered first and age is then added. Age does not explain a statistically significant amount of variation in recency beyond that accounted for by the utility structure index. It is concluded that the utility structure index explains the relationship between age and recency of use.

These analyses were repeated when considering recency of use and the attribute-time index. Table 8.9 shows the stepwise regression of the antecedent variables as measured for Round 1 on the Round 1 attribute-time index. Friend's use, age, and sociability are positively related to the index. As seen when comparing Tables 8.6 and 8.9, age is the only antecedent variable with relationships to both recency and the attribute-time index. Table 8.10 summarizes the regression in which the attribute-time index is entered first, and then age. Since age is not significantly related to recency after the index is entered, it is concluded that the attribute-time index accounts for the relationship between age and recency of use.

With regard to frequency of marijuana use, as seen in Table 8.11, three of the antecedent variables are significantly and positively related to frequency of use: friend's use, aspiration, and permissiveness. A comparison of Tables 8.7 and 8.11 indicates that friend's use is the only common correlate of the utility structure

TABLE 8.6

Stepwise Regression of the 19 Antecedent Variables as Measured
for Round 1 on Recency of Use as Measured for Round 2
(Sample: Users, Round 1; N = 103)

Independent Variables	Beta	B	Standard Error	R^2	F	p
Permissiveness	.315	.486	.140	.079	12.00	.0008
Aspiration	.236	.450	.175	.150	6.64	.0115
Age	.207	.498	.220	.192	5.13	.0250
Intercept	—	-2.006	—	—	—	—

Term	df	Mean Square	F	p
Regression	3	26.939	7.83	.0001
Error	99	3.441		

TABLE 8.7

Stepwise Regression of the 19 Antecedent Variables as Measured
for Round 1 on the Utility Structure Index as
Measured for Round 1
(Sample: Users, Round 1; N = 103)

Independent Variables	Beta	B	Standard Error	R^2	F	p
Friend's use	.249	193.851	64.436	.175	9.05	.0033
Age	.331	305.748	75.961	.235	16.20	.0001
Race	.299	753.982	214.652	.308	12.34	.0007
Sociability	.226	25.375	9.560	.332	7.04	.0093
Sex	-.177	-279.369	133.234	.361	4.40	.0386
Intercept	—	-3948.589	—	—	—	—

Term	df	Mean Square	F	p
Regression	5	4511568.656	10.98	.0001
Error	97	410853.706		

TABLE 8.8

Regression on Recency of Use as Measured for Round 2 with the
Utility Structure Index as Measured for Round 1 Entered First
and Age as Measured for Round 1 Entered Next
(Sample: Users, Round 1; N = 103)

Independent Variables	Beta	$\underline{B}$	Standard Error	R^2	$\underline{F}$	$\underline{p}$
Utility structure index	.384	.000999	.0002	.148	17.50	<.01
Intercept	—	5.9823	—	—	—	—
Variable that does not enter						
Age	.119	.286	.232	.161	1.53	N.S.

Term	$\underline{df}$	Mean Square	$\underline{F}$	$\underline{p}$
Regression	1	62.237	17.50	<.01
Error	101	3.557		

TABLE 8.9

Stepwise Regression of the 19 Antecedent Variables as Measured
for Round 1 on the Attribute-Time Index as Measured for Round 1
(Sample: Users, Round 1; N = 103)

Independent Variables	Beta	$\underline{B}$	Standard Error	R^2	$\underline{F}$	$\underline{p}$
Friend's use	.309	12.018	3.343	.123	12.93	.0005
Age	.298	13.796	3.965	.212	12.11	.0007
Sociability	.259	1.455	.482	.278	9.11	.0032
Intercept	—	-160.243	—	—	—	—

Term	$\underline{df}$	Mean Square	$\underline{F}$	$\underline{p}$
Regression	3	14536.417	12.73	.0001
Error	99	1141.776		

TABLE 8.10

Regression on Recency of Use as Measured for Round 2 with the
Attribute-Time Index as Measured for Round 1 Entered First
and Age as Measured for Round 1 Entered Next
(Sample: Users, Round 1; N = 103)

Independent Variable	Beta	B	Standard Error	R^2	F	p
Attribute-time index	.379	.0196	.005	.143	16.90	<.01
Intercept	—	6.06	—	—	—	—
Variable that does not enter						
Age	.117	.280	.233	.156	1.45	N.S.

Term	df	Mean Square	F	p
Regression	1	60.423	16.90	<.01
Error	101	3.574		

TABLE 8.11

Stepwise Regression of the 19 Antecedent Variables as Measured
for Round 1 on Frequency of Use as Measured for Round 2
(Sample: Users, Round 1; N = 103)

Independent Variables	Beta	B	Standard Error	R^2	F	p
Friend's use	.217	.399	.171	.071	5.42	.0219
Aspiration	.243	.420	.162	.118	6.76	.0108
Permissiveness	.209	.294	.130	.161	5.09	.0262
Intercept	—	-1.620	—	—	—	—

Term	df	Mean Square	F	p
Regression	3	18.781	6.35	.0006
Error	99	2.958		

index and frequency of use. Table 8.12 shows the results when entering the utility structure index first in a regression on frequency, and then friend's use. Friend's use is not significantly related to frequency under this condition, and therefore it is concluded that the utility structure index explains the relationship between that antecedent variable and frequency of use.

TABLE 8.12

Regression on Frequency of Use as Measured for Round 2 with the Utility Structure Index as Measured for Round 1 Entered First and Friend's Use as Measured for Round 1 Entered Next
(Sample: Users, Round 1; N = 103)

Independent Variable	Beta	B	Standard Error	R^2	F	p
Utility structure index	.350	.000829	.0002	.123	14.16	<.01
Intercept	—	3.622	—	—	—	—
Variable that does not enter Friend's use	.168	.309	.180	.148	2.95	N.S.

Term	df	Mean Square	F	p
Regression	1	42.929	14.16	<.01
Error	101	3.032		

Finally, considering the attribute index and frequency of use, the antecedent variables related to the attribute index are sociability, friend's use, age, and race (Table 8.13). Among these antecedent variables, the only common correlate with frequency of use (Table 8.11) is friend's use. Table 8.14 shows the results of regression on frequency in which the attribute index is entered first and then friend's use is added. Friend's use still explains a statistically significant amount of variance in frequency of use after the attribute index has been entered. It is concluded that the attribute index does not explain the relationship between friend's use and frequency of use of marijuana.

TABLE 8.13

Stepwise Regression of the 19 Antecedent Variables as Measured
for Round 1 on the Attribute Index as Measured for Round 1
(Sample: Users, Round 1; N = 103)

Independent Variables	Beta	B	Standard Error	R^2	F	p
Sociability	.216	.183	.075	.152	5.96	.0165
Friend's use	.242	1.417	.504	.197	7.92	.0059
Age	.268	1.867	.602	.239	9.63	.0025
Race	.264	5.004	1.690	.283	8.77	.0038
Intercept	—	−28.271	—	—	—	—

Term	df	Mean Square	F	p
Regression	4	250.680	9.69	.0001
Error	98	25.881		

TABLE 8.14

Regression on Frequency of Use as Measured for Round 2
with the Attribute Index as Measured for Round 1
Entered First and Friend's Use as Measured
for Round 1 Entered Next
(Sample: Users, Round 1; N = 103)

Independent Variables	Beta	B	Standard Error	R^2	F	p
Attribute index	.233	.073	.031	.084	5.63	<.05
Friend's use	.198	.364	.180	.120	4.08	<.05
Intercept	—	2.319	—	—	—	—

Term	df	Mean Square	F	p
Regression	2	20.957	6.82	<.01
Error	100	3.073		

CONCLUSION

The utility structure index does not show promise for explaining the relationships between most of the antecedent variables that were included for study and behavior with marijuana. For all analyses presented in this chapter, five or fewer antecedent variables from among the 19 were related in hypothesized directions with both the index and behavior, and when there were these common relationships, they often persisted after controlling for the index. However, the results also suggest that the indexes appear to be worthy of consideration as explanations for why perceived likelihood of attending college predicts subsequent use among non-users, why age is related to recency of use, and why friend's use is related to frequency of use.

9
THE UTILITY STRUCTURE AS
A CONSEQUENCE OF BEHAVIOR

Findings presented in Chapters 5, 6, and 7 support the hypothesis that the utility structure influences behavior with marijuana. The research was begun with the companion hypothesis that there might be a reciprocal relationship between the utility structure and behavior—that is, that the use of marijuana might be a determinant as well as a consequence of the utility structure. Perhaps as experience is gained through use of marijuana, some expected consequences are not matched by actual consequences, and as a result those attributes cease to be part of the utility structure. For example, a person might anticipate nausea from marijuana, not have nausea when using marijuana, and therefore that consequence might not be expected from future use of marijuana. Perhaps consequences occur from marijuana that were not expected, and they then become added to the utility structure. A person might not expect nausea from marijuana, have nausea after using it, and then add that attribute to the utility structure.

Moreover, the salience and subjective probability associated with attributes might change with behavior. "Getting high" might become more or less salient after using marijuana, and the perceived probability of feeling bad might increase or decrease depending upon what happened after using marijuana. This chapter represents the analyses designed to test the hypothesis that behavior with marijuana influences the utility structure.

ROUND 1 NONUSERS AND THEIR ROUND 2
UTILITY STRUCTURE

If behavior with marijuana influences the utility structure, then among those who reported on their Round 1 questionnaires that they had never used marijuana, the utility structure should change more for those who became users by Round 2 than for those who remained nonusers. The data in Figure 9.1, which make that comparison, are consistent with that hypothesis: the mean utility structure index changed more between Rounds 1 and 2 for those who became users between rounds than for those who remained nonusers. This analysis was repeated when using the attribute-subjective probability index rather than the utility structure index, since the analysis in Chapter 5 suggested that the components of salience and time were unnecessary for predicting behavior with marijuana for this group. The findings are shown in Figure 9.1 and the conclusions are the same as when using the utility structure index: the attribute-subjective probability index changed more for those who had used marijuana by Round 2 than for those who had not. Table 9.1 shows the means for these and the other indexes on both rounds, separately for those who did and did not use marijuana by Round 2. All changes are toward the positive; that is, there is a tendency for both those who became users and those who did not to become more favorably predisposed to use of marijuana. In each comparison the average change in the indexes between rounds was below 15 percent for those who did not use marijuana by Round 2, but among those who became users by Round 2 the change in the mean was 50 percent or greater across indexes.

This hypothesis, that use of marijuana influences the utility structure, was also tested by using analysis of covariance as an alternative analytical approach. Specifically, for those who said on their Round 1 questionnaires that they had never used marijuana, those who did and did not become users by Round 2 were compared on their Round 2 indexes when controlling for the Round 1 indexes. Controlling for the Round 1 indexes was necessary in this analysis because the groups differed on them, and it was desirable to remove these differences so that they did not influence the difference in indexes measured after the behavior with marijuana. The unadjusted and adjusted results are shown in Table 9.2. When controlling for the Round 1 indexes, there are statistically significant differences on their Round 2 indexes between those who did and did not use marijuana by Round 2. These findings are consistent with the conclusion that the use of marijuana has an influence on the utility structure.

ROUND 1 USERS AND THEIR ROUND 2
UTILITY STRUCTURE

Do the recency and frequency of use, as measured in Round 1 for those who indicated they had used marijuana, influence the Round 2 utility structure? When addressing this question, the hypothesis

FIGURE 9.1

Comparison of Round 2 Nonusers and Users on Round 1 and 2 Attribute–
Subjective Probability and Utility Structure Indexes
(Sample: Round 1 Nonusers)

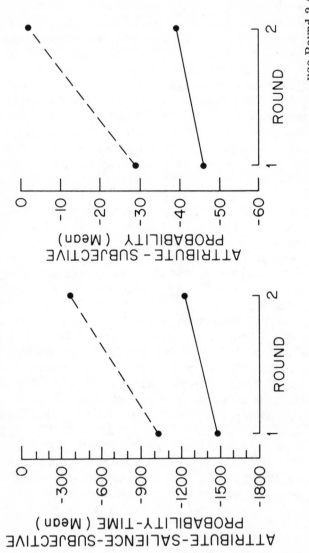

TABLE 9.1

Comparison of Round 2 Nonusers and Users on
Round 1 and Round 2 Indexes
(Sample: Round 1 Nonusers)

Index and Round 2 Use	Mean		Percent Change
	Round 1	Round 2	
Attribute			
Nonuse	-10.6	-9.6	9.4
Use	-7.1	-2.1	70.4
Attribute-salience			
Nonuse	-55.0	-51.2	6.9
Use	-39.9	-14.3	64.2
Attribute-subjective probability			
Nonuse	-46.4	-39.5	14.9
Use	-28.8	-2.1	92.7
Attribute-time			
Nonuse	-72.8	-67.4	7.4
Use	-53.2	-26.5	50.2
Attribute-salience- subjective probability			
Nonuse	-232.5	-206.3	11.3
Use	-156.0	-27.4	82.4
Attribute-salience-time			
Nonuse	-355.8	-337.3	5.2
Use	-268.2	-135.8	49.4
Attribute-subjective probability- time			
Nonuse	-305.6	-268.7	12.1
Use	-205.5	-65.8	68.0
Attribute-salience- subjective probability-time			
Nonuse	-1474.0	-1334.0	9.5
Use	-1023.9	-360.6	64.8

Notes: N for mean of each nonuse group = 759; N for mean of
each use group = 188. $p < .01$ (t-test) for each difference between
Round 1 and Round 2, and for each comparison between nonusers
and users within index and round.

TABLE 9.2

Comparison of Round 2 Users and Nonusers on Round 2 Indexes
(Sample: Round 1 Nonusers)

Index and Round 2 Use	Mean	
	Unadjusted	Adjusted for Round 1 Index
Attribute		
Nonuse	−9.6	−9.3
Use	−2.1	−3.2
Attribute-salience		
Nonuse	−51.2	−50.0
Use	−14.3	−19.1
Attribute-subjective probability		
Nonuse	−39.5	−38.2
Use	−2.1	−7.9
Attribute-time		
Nonuse	−67.4	−66.0
Use	−26.5	−32.3
Attribute-salience-subjective probability		
Nonuse	−206.3	−200.5
Use	−27.4	−50.9
Attribute-salience-time		
Nonuse	−337.3	−330.8
Use	−135.8	−162.2
Attribute-subjective probability-time		
Nonuse	−268.7	−261.3
Use	−65.8	−95.7
Attribute-salience-subjective probability-time		
Nonuse	−1334.0	−1300.4
Use	−360.6	−996.0

Notes: N for mean of each nonuse group = 759; N for mean of each use group = 188. $p < .01$ (t-test) for the difference between each unadjusted group, and $p < .01$ (covariance) for the difference between each group adjusted for Round 1 index.

that behavior with marijuana influences the utility structure is again being tested. Recency of use was first considered and the findings are presented in Table 9.3. There is a modest but statistically significant correlation between recency of use as measured in Round 1 and the Round 2 utility structure index (Column 1, bottom row, Table 9.3), and when considering four of the other indexes. All these correlations are in the expected direction of relatively positive utility structures for those who used marijuana most recently.

TABLE 9.3

Correlations between Round 1 Recency of Use and
Round 2 Indexes, and Partial Correlations
Controlling for Round 1 Indexes
(N = 131)

Index	Round 1 Recency by Round 2 Index	Round 1 Recency by Round 2 Index, Partial for Round 1 Index
Attribute	.12	.06
Attribute-salience	.18*	.08
Attribute-subjective probability	.16*	.08
Attribute-time	.12	.04
Attribute-salience-subjective probability	.18*	.08
Attribute-salience-time	.17*	.09
Attribute-subjective probability-time	.12	.06
Attribute-salience-subjective probability-time	.16*	.08

*$p < .05$ (Pearson $\underline{r}$).

For each of these relationships between Round 1 recency of use and Round 2 index partial correlations were calculated to control for the Round 1 index. This control was introduced because the Round 1 and Round 2 indexes are correlated—there is a statistically significant correlation at $p < .01$ between Round 1 and Round 2 for each index, with correlations ranging from .23 to .29 across indexes—and therefore correlations between Round 1 behavior and Round 2 index could be a reflection of the correlations between the Round 1 and 2 indexes. The question here is whether behavior rather than the Round 1 index predicts the Round 2 index. The partial correlations are shown in the second column of Table 9.3. For each index, when relating Round 1 recency with the Round 2 index and controlling for the Round 1 index, the correlation is not statistically significant. This suggests that Round 1 recency of use does not influence the Round 2 utility structure independently of the Round 1 utility structure.

These analyses were repeated when considering frequency of use as measured in Round 1. The results, shown in Table 9.4, are identical to those described for recency of use. It is concluded that Round 1 frequency of use is related to the Round 2 indexes, but that this is attributable to the Round 1 indexes.

TABLE 9.4

Correlations between Round 1 Frequency of Use and
Round 2 Indexes, and Partial Correlations
Controlling for Round 1 Indexes
(N = 131)

Index	Round 1 Frequency by Round 2 Index	Round 1 Frequency by Round 2 Index, Partial for Round 1 Index
Attribute	.16*	.02
Attribute-salience	.16*	.06
Attribute-subjective probability	.13	.04
Attribute-time	.12	.04
Attribute-salience-subjective probability	.16*	.06
Attribute-salience-time	.17*	.09
Attribute-subjective probability-time	.13	.06
Attribute-salience-subjective probability-time	.17*	.08

*$p < .05$ (Pearson r).

CONCLUSION

The findings are consistent with the hypothesis that among those who have never used marijuana, the utility structure becomes more positive among those who use marijuana one year later. This is not definitive proof that behavior influences the utility structure, because the utility structure as measured for Round 2 might have actually changed before the change in behavior between rounds and thereby influenced that behavior. Thus, the behavior might not have influenced the utility structure. There is no way to pinpoint from the data exactly when the Round 2 utility structure and behavior changed. However, had the differences between those who did and did not use marijuana by Round 2 as shown in Figure 9.1 and Table 9.1 not appeared, that would have been considered sufficient evidence against the hypothesis that behavior influences the utility structure. No relationships were found between Round 1 recency or frequency of use with the Round 2 indexes, when controlling for the Round 1 indexes. It is concluded that among users, these behaviors do not have an influence on the indexes as measured one year later.

10
REDUCING THE NUMBER OF ATTRIBUTES

INTRODUCTION

The anticipated consequences included in the indexes used in all preceding analyses were chosen through literature review and pilot study. However, some of the attributes included in the indexes may have been unnecessary for predicting subsequent behavior with marijuana. Theoretical parsimony could be gained by eliminating the unnecessary consequences. Moreover, elimination of unnecessary attributes could have methodological and practical advantages. Use of fewer consequences in future research could reduce subject boredom and fatigue that might occur when subjects are asked to provide information related to 54 consequences, and their consideration of fewer consequences might thereby enhance measurement accuracy. And, with fewer consequences and limited data collection time with each subject, more detailed questions might be asked than those used in the questionnaire. More rigorous measurement strategies might also be possible with fewer consequences. For example, it would have been preferable to have subjects make direct comparisons among combinations of positive and negative consequences. This was impossible with 54 consequences initially identified as necessary for study and only 90 minutes with each subject each time data were collected. From the pragmatic view, a program or policy that focuses upon the consequences of behavior might be more cost effective if only the attributes critical for behavior are considered. Thus, for example, if the consequences of drug behavior are the focus of a school education or mass media program, it might be most cost effective to focus upon the dozen or so consequences that predict behavior than to deal with these plus many more that do not relate to behavior when included in the utility structure.

This chapter presents and assesses a procedure for reducing the number of anticipated consequences in an index of utility. The components of delayed consequence and time orientation are ignored in these analyses for two basic reasons. First, measures of time typically failed to add to the explained variance in behavior in analyses presented in earlier chapters, and when they did, their addition was small. Second, the index that remains without the component for time is most analogous to the measures of subjective expected utility (SEU) used in the most recent field studies of utility. In this latter regard, it was felt that this method would prove more useful to other studies if the focus was on SEU.

As described in Chapter 5, the SEU index is formed for each subject by first multiplying the score for each attribute (1 = chosen, 0 = not chosen) by the product of the companion scores for salience (1 = unimportant to 5 = very very important) and subjective probability (1 = impossible to 5 = absolutely certain), then summing these products for the positive and negative consequences separately, and finally subtracting the sum of the negative from the sum of the positive. This measure has, of course, appeared in most of the preceding chapters in which findings were presented, and is very strongly correlated with each of the other indexes.

A METHOD FOR ELIMINATING ATTRIBUTES

The key feature of the method for reducing the number of attributes is that it derives from the fundamental assumption that attributes with high salience and high subjective probability are more important to SEU than attributes with low salience and low subjective probability. A person must consider peer approval to be an important and probable consequence of using marijuana in order for that attribute to make a substantial contribution to the SEU. This is reflected by the measure of SEU that gives attributes with high salience and high subjective probability more weight than attributes with low salience and low subjective probability. With this basic feature as a guide, attributes that are ascribed either low salience or low subjective probability by relatively many subjects are eliminated, and those attributes that are assigned both high salience and high subjective probability by relatively many people are retained for a measure of SEU.

Before inspecting the data in a fashion that allowed identification of the percentage of people who ascribed high salience and subjective probability to attributes, a criterion was set: subjects must score 3 or higher on both salience and subjective probability on an attribute (they had to consider the consequence at least "somewhat important" and "somewhat likely") in order for that attribute to be considered high on salience and subjective probability for the subject. Table 10.1 shows the percent of subjects who reported on their Round 1 questionnaires that they had never used marijuana and scored high on salience and subjective probability on the attribute, with the attributes listed in descending order of the percents. Thus, as seen from the table, 29.6 percent assigned high salience and high subjective probability to "worry less," 27.6 percent to "feel happier," and so forth. The percents for Round 1 users are shown in Table 10.2.

It was decided that a minimum of five positive and five negative attributes must be included in the index with the reduced number of attributes. This minimum number of items was established by assuming that at least five are desirable for satisfactory reliability of measurement, and because behavior with marijuana and most other choice behavior is so complex that at least that many positive and negative attributes are important. The second stipulation was that attributes that did not have a statistically significant difference from the fifth attribute on the list would be added beyond the first five when using the McNemar test for the difference in proportions between dependent samples. The reasoning was that the fifth attribute and those lower on the list that were not significantly different from the fifth were in the same domain, at least from the standpoint of statistical significance. When applying these criteria the attributes designated by asterisks in Tables 10.1 and 10.2 are considered high on salience and subjective probability by relatively large numbers of subjects.

By this method the number of attributes is substantially reduced, from the 54 positive and negative consequences in the original set, to 12 and 16 for the samples of Round 1 nonusers and users, respectively. These attributes are then used to form an index as described above for SEU, except that a majority of the attributes—those not designated by an asterisk in Tables 10.1 or 10.2—are excluded from this index. This index is called SEU HIGH, and the original index with all 54 consequences, SEU TOTAL.

ASSESSMENT OF THE METHOD

To evaluate the procedure for eliminating attributes from a measure of SEU, SEU HIGH and SEU TOTAL are used. A third index is also used—SEU LOW—which is calculated in the same manner as SEU TOTAL and SEU HIGH except that SEU LOW includes only the attributes that were eliminated. In all the analyses Round 1 data are used for the SEU measures. When behavior is introduced

TABLE 10.1

Percent of Subjects High on Round 1 Salience and Subjective Probability (Round 1 Nonusers)

(N = 947)

Positive Attributes	Percent	Negative Attributes	Percent
*Worry less	29.6	*Do strange or dangerous things, lose control over myself	75.2
*Feel happier	27.6	*Be arrested by the police	73.4
*Feel more pleasure	21.4	*Get into trouble with parents	72.3
*Be less bored	20.9	*Get into trouble with the police	68.6
*Be more relaxed	18.9	*Go on to more harmful drugs	68.2
*Satisfy my curiosity	18.1	*Not be able to stop using drugs	67.3
Feel at home with the group	13.9	Be a bad example for others	64.4
Enjoy doing things with my friends	12.1	Go to jail	63.5
Have less pain	11.9	Not be able to think as well	61.1
Have other kids think that I am cool	11.5	Feel bad	61.0
Get high	9.9	Cause accidents	59.5
Have different or interesting thoughts	8.7	Feel like I am going crazy	58.2
Have more self-confidence	7.9	Die from an overdose	58.2
Be liked more by my friends or have more friends	7.7	Harm my body forever	58.0
Feel more important or grown-up	7.0	Feel guilty because it is against the law, or my religion, or my morals	47.3
Enjoy the taste	6.2	Get into trouble with people who sell drugs	45.4
Feel closer to others	5.8	Get into trouble with the teacher or principal	45.2
Sleep better	5.8	Not be able to do things such as running or walking as well	43.3
Feel stronger	5.3	Be liked less by friends or have fewer friends	42.8
Act against my parents, other adults, or society	4.1	Become more nervous	41.1
Understand myself better	4.0	Have to spend too much money	40.2
Feel as if time were passing slower	2.9	Not live as long	39.2
Be able to do things better	2.7	Lose respect for myself	38.7
See, smell, taste, hear or feel things better	2.0	Lose interest in things	33.7
Help me control my weight	1.4	Be less understanding of myself	30.2
Be able to think better	1.3	Be sadder	18.4
		Feel as if time were passing slower	13.5
		Dislike the taste	10.9

*Attributes selected for SEU HIGH.

TABLE 10.2

Percent of Subjects High on Round 1 Salience and Subjective Probability (Round 1 Users)

(N = 131)

Positive Attributes	Percent	Negative Attributes	Percent
*Feel more pleasure	68.7	*Get into trouble with parents	46.7
*Feel happier	58.8	*Be arrested by the police	44.3
*Be more relaxed	51.9	*Get into trouble with the police	39.7
*Be less bored	48.2	*Go to jail	35.1
*Worry less	48.1	*Do strange or dangerous things, lose control over myself	32.9
*Get high	42.0	*Have to spend too much money	29.8
Enjoy doing things with my friends	35.9	*Not be able to think as well	29.1
Feel at home with the group	26.8	*Go on to more harmful drugs	26.8
Satisfy my curiosity	25.2	*Cause accidents	26.0
Have less pain	23.9	*Not be able to stop using drugs	25.3
Enjoy the taste	21.4	Be a bad example for others	22.2
Feel closer to others	20.0	Feel bad	20.7
Be liked more by my friends or have more friends	20.0	Get into trouble with the teacher or principal	20.6
Sleep better	19.2	Die from an overdose	19.2
Have other kids think that I am cool	17.6	Get into trouble with people who sell drugs	19.1
Have different or interesting thoughts	16.2	Harm my body forever	17.6
Have more self-confidence	14.6	Not be able to do things such as running or walking as well	16.3
Feel more important or grown-up	10.8	Not live as long	16.0
Feel stronger	9.9	Become more nervous	15.3
Understand myself better	9.3	Feel guilty because it is against the law, or my religion, or my morals	15.3
Feel as if time were passing slower	6.2	Lose interest in things	14.6
Act against my parents, other adults or society	6.2	Feel like I am going crazy	14.5
See, smell, taste, hear or feel things better	5.3	Be liked less by friends or have fewer friends	13.1
Be able to do things better	4.8	Lose respect for myself	12.3
Be able to think better	4.6	Feel as if time were passing slower	8.6
Help me control my weight	3.1	Be less understanding of myself	6.9
		Be sadder	4.7
		Dislike the taste	3.2

*Attributes selected for SEU HIGH.

as a variable, all analyses are done separately for Round 1 nonusers and users. When Round 1 nonusers are the portion of the sample in the analysis, then the dependent variable is whether marijuana had been used as reported on the Round 2 questionnaire. When Round 1 users are the sample of study, the dependent variable is either the recency or frequency of marijuana use as measured in Round 2.

Correlation matrixes for the three SEU indexes are shown in Table 10.3. There is a statistically significant relationship between each pair of indexes for both Round 1 nonusers and users. And, for both nonusers and users, the correlations between SEU HIGH and SEU LOW are weaker than the correlations between either SEU HIGH or SEU LOW and SEU TOTAL. Thus, although each of the indexes with the smaller number of attributes is a strong correlate of SEU TOTAL, the correlations between the two reduced indexes are so weak that they might not be acceptable substitutes for each other.

TABLE 10.3

Correlations between Round 1 SEU Measures

	Round 1 Nonusers (N = 947)			Round 1 Users (N = 131)		
	SEU HIGH	SEU LOW	SEU TOTAL	SEU HIGH	SEU LOW	SEU TOTAL
SEU HIGH	1.00	—	—	1.00	—	—
SEU LOW	.70	1.00	—	.69	1.00	—
SEU TOTAL	.83	.98	1.00	.90	.93	1.00

Note: All correlations have $p < .05$ (Pearson r).

Table 10.4 shows the correlations between each SEU index and behavior. For both nonusers and users there is a statistically significant relationship in the predicted direction between each of the indexes and subsequent behavior. However, there are no statistically significant differences between correlations within the nonuser and user groups. That SEU HIGH, SEU LOW, and SEU TOTAL have the same correlations with behavior suggests, as did the correlations among indexes shown in Table 10.3, that both SEU HIGH and SEU LOW might be satisfactorily substituted for SEU TOTAL, and in this sense parsimony has been achieved, since both SEU HIGH and SEU LOW contain substantially fewer attributes than SEU TOTAL.

TABLE 10.4

Correlations between Round 1 SEU Measures
and Round 2 Behavior

	Round 1 Nonusers (N = 947)	Round 1 Users and Recency (N = 131)	Round 1 Users and Frequency (N = 131)
SEU HIGH	.21	.36	.35
SEU LOW	.19	.28	.27
SEU TOTAL	.21	.34	.34

Notes: All correlations have p < .05 (Pearson r). Within the three sections of the table there are no statistically significant differences between correlations.

There is an inclination to choose SEU HIGH over SEU LOW because the former contains fewer attributes than the latter. However, for two reasons the inclination is an unsatisfactory criterion for choosing between SEU HIGH and SEU LOW. First, SEU HIGH and SEU LOW contain different attributes, and for the theoretical, methodological, and practical reasons given for developing this method, it is necessary to be reasonably certain that the set of attributes is appropriate. For example, to reduce measurement error it is preferable to refine measures for appropriate rather than inappropriate attributes in a measure of SEU. Therefore, it is necessary to assess the relative merits of SEU HIGH and SEU LOW with rigor. Second, the basic theoretical rationale for this method is that SEU HIGH should be preferable to SEU LOW because SEU HIGH contains attributes to which relatively many people ascribed high salience and high subjective probability when compared with the attributes in SEU LOW. The assessment thus far has not revealed evidence that SEU HIGH is the preferred index, and therefore the basic assumption of the method could be incorrect.

To choose between SEU HIGH and SEU LOW correlations were calculated between SEU HIGH and behavior when partialing for SEU LOW, and correlations between SEU LOW and behavior when partialing for SEU HIGH. If SEU HIGH is the method of choice over SEU LOW, as suggested by the reasoning for the method, then when partialing for SEU LOW a statistically significant relationship between SEU HIGH and behavior should remain, and when partialing for SEU HIGH the relationship between SEU LOW and behavior should

TABLE 10.5

First-Order and Partial Correlations of SEU HIGH and SEU LOW Round 1 with Round 2 Behavior

	Round 1 Nonusers (N = 947)	Round 1 Users (N = 131)	Round 1 Users (N = 131)
SEU HIGH and USE		**SEU HIGH and Recency**	**SEU HIGH and Frequency**
Zero-order	.21*	.36*	.35*
Partial for SEU LOW	.11*	.24*	.23*
SEU LOW and USE		**SEU LOW and Recency**	**SEU LOW and Frequency**
Zero-order	.19*	.28*	.27*
Partial for SEU HIGH	.06 n.s.	.04 n.s.	.05 n.s.

Note: * = p < .05 (Pearson r̲).

113

be significantly reduced. The first-order and partial correlations
are shown in Table 10.5. Using the criteria established for inter-
preting the partial correlations, it is concluded that SEU HIGH is
the index choice: when partialing for SEU LOW, statistically significant relationships between SEU HIGH and behavior remain,
whereas when partialing for SEU HIGH, the relationship between
SEU LOW and behavior is reduced to zero. This occurs for both
Round 1 nonusers and users, and for both behavior variables among
users. The conclusion is that the method yields the reduced measure of SEU that is most compatible with the theory.

DISCUSSION

These analyses suggest the positive and negative attributes
most important to the SEU of relatively large numbers of the subjects. When considering those subjects who were nonusers at the
time of Round 1 (Table 10.1), the most important positive consequences for the largest part of the sample are those that are expected to bring direct and immediate psychological or physical satisfaction: less worry, less boredom, increased relaxation, and
satisfaction of curiosity. Positive attributes that were considered
to be of low salience and subjective probability by relatively many
of the subjects—and hence assumed to be of lesser SEU importance—
include such frequent explanations for drug use as being liked more
by friends, feeling more important or grown-up, feeling closer to
others, and acting out against others. The negative consequences
assigned high salience and subjective probability by relatively many
of the Round 1 nonusers were the fear of doing strange or dangerous
things and loss of control, negative sanctions by the police and parents, use of more harmful drugs, and addiction. Negative consequences chosen to have high salience and subjective probability by
relatively few subjects include such frequent explanations for not
using drugs as loss of self-respect, getting in trouble at school,
and being liked less by friends or having fewer friends.
When considering the Round 1 users and their positive consequences (Table 10.2), the attributes of high salience and subjective
probability by the largest part of the sample are strikingly similar
to those for Round 1 nonusers: feeling more pleasure, increased
happiness, more relaxation, less boredom, less worry, and getting
high. Similar to Round 1 nonusers, the Round 1 users were relatively unlikely to ascribe high salience and subjective probability to
such positive consequences as acting out against others, feeling
more important or grown-up, and enhanced self-understanding.
Round 2 users were also relatively likely to assign high salience

and subjective probability to such negative consequences as sanctions by parents and police, doing strange or dangerous things and losing control over self, using more harmful drugs, and becoming addicted. The economic cost of drugs, not being able to think as well, and causing accidents also survived the researchers' cutoff of negative consequences for Round 1 users. Such negative consequences chosen by relatively few Round 1 users were such common explanations for not using drugs as being less liked by friends or having fewer friends, losing respect, and negative psychological consequences.

This method was developed for use after the collection of the final data in the research. However, it or a variation of it might also be considered for use at a much earlier stage of research. When conducting literature reviews and pilot studies to identify attributes to be measured in the research on marijuana behavior, more attributes were found than could be tolerated either by the amount of time available for administering questionnaires to the subjects or by the patience of some of the pilot subjects. Those attributes that were already encompassed by other attributes were excluded from the final measures. It is possible that this might have been done more systematically, and fewer attributes generated for study, if the criteria of the method developed for elimination of attributes had been used on pilot data. Thus, measurement might have been improved for the final data through more refined measurement of the smaller number of attributes. It is recommended that the method be considered for a priori as well as ex post facto elimination of attributes.

The procedure for reducing the number of anticipated consequences can be easily altered to meet the particular needs of other studies. For example, analyses presented in earlier chapters suggest that the components of salience and subjective probability add either nothing or minor amounts to the prediction of behavior by SEU. Thus, when the attributes are rank ordered according to the percent of subjects who chose them, and salience and subjective probability are ignored, the order is quite similar to that presented in Tables 10.1 and 10.2, when salience and subjective probability were included. Since other field studies of SEU typically include measures at least roughly equivalent to salience and subjective probability, for illustrative purposes those components were included in the analysis. Moreover, other studies may find it appropriate to establish different cutting points for determining whether consequences are of high salience and subjective probability, and for deciding how many attributes should be included in an index of SEU.

CONCLUSION

The number of attributes in a measure of SEU can be substantially reduced by retaining those consequences that are considered to be of high salience and high subjective probability by relatively many subjects. Reducing the number of attributes has the potential for enhancing theoretical parsimony, improving measurement, and identifying consequences of relatively great practical significance.

11
CONCLUSIONS AND IMPLICATIONS

This chapter summarizes the results of this study, mentions several of the caveats that must accompany the conclusions, and considers the implications of the research for future studies of marijuana behavior, programs and policies related to the prevention of drug behavior, and other behavior that involves individual choice.

CONCLUSIONS AND CAVEATS

The analyses consistently revealed statistically significant relationships between the various measures of utility and subsequent behavior with marijuana. All these relationships were in the hypothesized direction of increased use of marijuana as the utility for marijuana became more positive. The magnitude of the relationships between utility and behavior fared quite favorably, relative to most earlier etiological studies of marijuana behavior, and when compared with the correlations between marijuana use and the antecedent variables included in this research. The study began with the hypothesis that all components of the utility structure would be necessary for explaining marijuana behavior, but the strong correlations among indexes containing different combinations of components precluded some of them from adding to the explanation of marijuana use. As hypothesized, the data were consistent with the conclusion that behavior with marijuana might influence utility. A few of the findings supported the general hypothesis that the utility measures accounted for the relationships between some antecedent variables and marijuana behavior, but support of this hypothesis was typically an exception and not the rule. The assessment of a method for reducing the number of attributes in a measure of subjective expected utility suggested that fewer attributes could have been used without a significant reduction in the prediction of marijuana use. That all the findings derived from a panel design, and that they held generally for two different groups in the sample (nonusers and users at Round 1) and different dependent variables (ever use, recency of use, and frequency of use) strengthens the confidence of the researchers in these conclusions, and the inference that causal connections exist between utility and the use of marijuana in the sample.

As for any research endeavor, there are some cautionary notes. First, most of the findings derive from slightly under half of the subjects that were initially intended to be in the study, and how attrition might influence the generalizability of the findings is not known. Second, although the study locale was quite similar to the United States as a whole on several sociodemographic indicators, one cannot be certain that the findings can be automatically generalized to all other populations. Third, the subjects provided data when they were seventh and eighth graders, and although the theoretical framework contains no restrictions on grade level, it is always possible that the findings would have been different for younger or older people. Finally, although it is inferred from the findings that causal relationships were observed between the various measures of utility and subsequent behavior in the sample, the problem that most of the behavior in the sample remains unexplained is shared with all other studies of marijuana behavior. These qualifications apply to all findings presented in earlier chapters and to the discussion that constitutes the remainder of this book.

The final caveat mentioned above—that most of the variance in marijuana behavior remained unexplained by the utility measures—requires elaboration. There are several possible reasons for this outcome. Perhaps variables other than those reflected by the indexes of utility are more important proximal determinants of marijuana behavior. The identification and measurement of such variables are left to the efforts of other investigators, and they are encouraged to attempt this because their success would add to the explanation of marijuana behavior. Moreover, if there are other proximal determinants to be identified, then their consideration by research could address the speculation that is typically employed to account for relationships between more distal antecedent variables and behavior. For example, measurement and analyses that involve the variables that might intervene between peer use and drug behavior would seem more valuable than speculation about the variables that might serve as the link. The amount of variance in behavior explained might also have been reduced by the length of the interval between Round 1 and Round 2 measures. A one-year interval was chosen because that was the lag necessary to provide sufficient change in marijuana behavior, given the number of cases it was possible to study. However, since the utility indexes changed substantially for the subjects during the one year—for example, the correlations between Round 1 and Round 2 indexes for Round 1 users were less than .30 (Chapter 9)—this could only serve to reduce the strength of relationships between Round 1 measures of utility and Round 2 behavior, and a shorter interval might have substantially enhanced predictability. Finally, perhaps much of the variance in behavior remained unexplained as a result of the measurement error in the utility variables. Ways to refine these measures are suggested in the next section of this chapter.

FUTURE RESEARCH

The findings clearly indicate that the utility structure, or some variant of this variable, is worthy of consideration in future studies of the determinants of marijuana behavior. Several refinements in measures of the utility variables, which might enhance the amount of variance in marijuana behavior that is explained, are offered here.

Even though some of the components of the utility structure did not add to the explanation of behavior in the data—most consistent in this regard was salience, and for some analyses either time or subjective probability—these measures might be improved. For example, in more recent studies subjects are being asked to indicate directly whether they consider a consequence would be accrued immediately or in the future, rather than relying on the assessment of judges other than the research subjects. The validity of the time orientation measure might be worthy of study, and although during pilot studies the measures of salience and subjective probability appeared to be tapping the dimensions that were considered essential, this is not tantamount to declaring that they are incapable of further refinement. As others have concluded (see, for example, Fishbein and Azjen 1975), there can be subtle but fundamental conceptual differences between the variables chosen to represent the components, and this can influence the amount of variance explained in behavior. Moreover, if some components are being considered by subjects when making judgments about other components—for example, time is considered when assessing salience or subjective probability— then measurement of some components is unnecessary. If future studies improve upon these measures and still find limited support for the value of some components for predicting behavior, then they should be deleted from future theoretical and research consideration.

The number of attributes considered in research might be reduced, perhaps through use of procedures described in the preceding chapter. Given limited data collection time with subjects, and especially subjects as young as those in this study, exposure to many attributes might produce more error than desirable through reduction in subject concentration. The practicalities of data collection also limit the amount of detail that can be obtained for each of many attributes. Moreover, as indicated in earlier chapters, a reduction in the number of attributes could facilitate the use of more acceptable levels of measurement for the variable. For example, with fewer attributes, methods might be developed that would allow subjects to make comparisons among various combinations of attributes directly in such ways that interval or ratio level of measurement could be approximated for the utility variables. This refinement in measurement has the potential for adding to the amount of variance explained in behavior. Finally, it is presumed that more sophisticated measurement will be possible when subjects are older than those in this study, when there is more data collection time for each subject, and when interviews rather than self-administered questionnaires can be used.

Also, as indicated earlier, more variance in marijuana behavior might be explained through shorter time intervals between measurement of the utility variables and behavior. And, of course, the measures of other variables—both the antecedent and the dependent variables—are not completely free of error, and reduction of that error could contribute directly to the strength of correlations among variables.

PROGRAMS AND POLICIES

In considering the research in the context of programs and policies that relate to the prevention of drug use, it should be noted that these programs and policies typically encompass many drugs, and therefore this discussion is not limited to marijuana.

All programs and policies deal in some central way with the consequences of drugs. Perhaps the most common method used in an attempt to influence drug behavior is to inform people about the harmful consequences that can be accrued. There is a wide range of examples of this approach, including drug education programs in schools, counseling programs designed to reduce drug use, the majority of films dealing with drugs, TV campaigns with the pitfalls of drug use as content, and the warning that death may result from a combination of drugs and driving. In terms of utility this is seen as an attempt to have the prospective drug user assimilate negative consequences that outweigh the positive, and through that mechanism not use drugs, or consume them with moderation. Many of these programs can also be viewed as attempts to increase salience or subjective probability associated with drug behavior, and thus serve as a means to influence behavior. Being a drug user can be presented as "wrecking the family," and that might be seen as an attempt to increase the salience of the intact family.

The negative emphasis approach in drug abuse education remains the one most commonly used, but it is falling into disrepute (see, for example, Wald and Abrams 1972; Weimar 1972; Vogl 1970; Halleck 1970; Zanowiak 1970; Levy 1971). One reason for the waning popularity of this approach is that it has been tried, and yet drug use continues to increase. The version of utility theory set forth here would explain this program failure by hypothesizing that for many individuals the expected positive consequences continue to outweigh the negative, even when emphasis is placed upon the negative. Perhaps some positive consequences, such as relief from tension and having a good time, are assigned such strong degrees of salience that for some individuals the negative consequences accrued through such information programs simply do not tip the scales in favor of the negative. Perhaps time orientation dilutes some of the anticipated negative consequences. For example, the present-oriented individual simply does not have drug behavior influenced by such future events as illness caused by drugs; or perhaps the probabilities associated with illness are simply too low for the expected negative consequences, even though emphasized in the curriculum, so that for many people the negatives do not outweigh the positive.

Another reason provided for the waning support of the approach that emphasizes negative consequences is that failure to recognize the positive consequences of drugs provokes a credibility gap between the information provider and the recipient (Vogl 1970; Halleck 1970). Audiences are composed of persons who have either received positive consequences from drugs, or know others who have reported positive consequences, and this conflicts with a factual accounting of only the negative consequences of drug use. Regardless of the explanation given for the trend away from this approach to influencing drug behavior, it is being questioned as a method and can be framed in terms of utility theory.

Thus, newer approaches are being tried to influence behavior. One is to provide information about the positive as well as negative consequences. This is intended to reduce the credibility gap between the provider and the recipient of information. Moreover, it fits within the rational model that individuals should be presented all facts relevant to making decisions, and regardless of their decisions, when they make them, they will be informed decisions. (See, for example, Weimar 1972; Levy 1971.) In terms of utility, instill perceptions of both positive and negative consequences and the individual will then be in the position to make an informed decision regarding personal behavior. Another approach receiving increased emphasis in an attempt to influence drug behavior is called "drug alternatives." Although this approach has been formulated in a variety of ways (National Institute on Drug Abuse 1974), basic to most of them is the notion that there are positive consequences that can be acquired through drugs, and if these are provided through other means—such as acquiring excitement through athletics or peer acceptance through peer organizations—drugs will not be used. In the language of utility, provide the good effects of drugs through activities other than drugs, and then the negative consequences will outweigh the positive consequences expected from drugs and drug behavior will be influenced accordingly.

Another trend for programs designed to influence drug behavior is based upon the assumption that the behavior is a symptom of social and psychological problems that must be treated through such procedures as group therapy and counseling (see Ungerleider and Bowen 1969; Levy 1971). For example, the propensity to consume drugs is seen as a reflection of parent-child conflict, psychological stress, or peer group pressures that must be changed to influence behavior, and counseling or group therapy might produce the change. Or, perhaps education programs in the schools should be conducted within the context of attempting to influence total mental health. The present version of utility theory suggests this approach may be successful if the utility structure is changed to a sufficient degree in the process of treating the social and psychological variables, since the utility structure is viewed as intervening between those variables and drug behavior.

These examples should suffice to indicate how utility theory applies in the context of programs designed to influence drug behavior. It is also applicable with regard to legislation related to drugs. Implicit in the presumed effect of laws designed to minimize drug use is the idea that the anticipated consequence of being apprehended and punished deters use of drugs. However, in spite of this, many young people use drugs. The utility theory explanation would take the following form. The anticipated consequence "legal sanction" is only one of many associated with drugs, and to consider it alone ignores the possibility that positive consequences are also associated with drugs. If the positive outweigh the negative, then the individual will use drugs. If, on the other hand, the negative outweigh the positive, the individual will not use drugs. Moreover, subjective probability, salience, and time orientation may play a role. Some may perceive the probability of legal complications through drug use to be quite low, and therefore that consequence would play a less important role in behavior than for the individual who has a higher subjective probability for incurring that negative consequence. Or individuals may assign different degrees of salience to legal sanction from drug use, and that, when considered with other anticipated consequences, may produce different patterns of drug behavior. Or individuals oriented toward the present may not give much weight to a jail sentence that would be seen as too far in the future to influence more immediate behavior.

Innumerable other examples could be used to show how utility theory can be applied to programs and policies related to drug behavior. The common theme for this consideration of programs and policies related to drug behavior, as conceptualized from the utility viewpoint, is diagrammed in Figure 11.1. Thus, programs and policies can be viewed as having an influence on drug behavior through their impact on utility. If the causes of the behavior are influenced enough by programs and policies, then the behavior will change.

The findings show some but not substantial support for this model. Policies and programs could have profound effects for utility, but if utility and behavior are modestly rather than strongly related, the ultimate impact on drug behavior will be small or non-existent. This poses a problem in considering the relevance of the findings for policies and programs because it is not possible to determine whether the modest, though statistically significant, relationships between utility and behavior exist because utility is a minor determinant, or whether the relationship is reduced by measurement error, the time interval between the measures, or some other factor. If utility is not an important proximal determinant of drug behavior—and programs and policies are designed to influence utility—then this could explain why programs and policies are less effective than intended. Further research is needed for the resolution of this uncertainty.

CHOICE BEHAVIOR

The version of the theory described in Chapter 1 that stimulated this study can be viewed in the context of any behavior that allows individual choice, such as use of drugs other than marijuana, eating too much or too little, voting for or against a bond issue, sexual activity, and following a doctor's prescription. That earlier chapter cited studies that share many of the elements of this version of the theory and other types of behavior. When considering different behaviors it is assumed that different sets of consequences are appropriate. Becoming an alcoholic might be an anticipated consequence of drinking alcohol, but it is probably not a consequence to be expected from voting for or against a school bond issue. Moreover, even when different behaviors share a consequence, the

FIGURE 11.1

Policies and Programs, Utility, and Drug Behavior

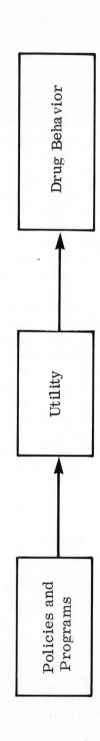

distributions of people according to the components may be different. For example, pleasure might be expected both from eating and from drinking alcohol, but the perceived probability of receiving pleasure from these activities might vary for many people. Aside from these changes necessary to account for the nature of consequences associated with specific behaviors, it is suspected that the theory would read pretty much the same for all behaviors that involve individual choice.

That most behavior involves individual choice makes this framework particularly appealing for the study of behavior. The fact that many different disciplines have theories that are based upon the importance of the benefits and costs of behavior to understanding behavior—even though different labels may be given to the theories and their features may vary across theories and disciplines—further enhances the appeal of the utility variable for understanding behavior. However, as indicated above when considering future research, programs, and policies, it is necessary to identify stronger correlations between the utility variables and behavior than found by this study before utility can be more enthusiastically endorsed as an important explanation for behavior. Thus, there is less enthusiasm than that expressed by Jeremy Bentham (1780) who declared long ago that the weighing of pleasure and pain is critical to understanding all behavior, but it is certainly fair to conclude from the results of this research that this principle is very worthy of further investigation.

Two other comments need to be made here. First, there is sometimes a tendency to assume from theoretical frameworks, such as the one used here, that people, when not involved in research, must expand substantial time and effort in making detailed calculations of utilities each time they make a decision in order for the theory to be of worth. For example, it is assumed that people must sit down with pencil and paper, list their consequences, and calculate subjective probabilities before subtracting the negative from the positive when making any decision. For most behaviors it simply does not work that way; that is, this process appears to be much less precise. The present research suggests that roughly analogous calculations can be made for some cases after they have provided the necessary information, and that their behavior with marijuana can then be predicted. The worth of the theory does not depend upon people behaving in an overtly calculating manner.

Second, it is sometimes taken for granted that utility or similar variables, such as attitudes, are proximal determinants of behavior, and since this is so obvious their relationships with behavior need not be addressed by research. In other words, it should be assumed that the strong correlations between utility and behavior exist, and therefore it is unecessary to include them among the variables measured in research. Although there are a number of arguments against this reasoning, in the context of this study it is difficult to reconcile with the fact that those variables were included and most of the variance in the behavior of interest was left unexplained. It is hoped that future research will include measures of utility, and through methodological improvements enhance the amount of variance explained by these variables.

FINAL NOTE

The findings in this study provide substantial support for the potential value of conducting future research on the relationship between utility and behavior. However, the findings have not been used to provide detailed and definitive directions for programs and policies, and the research is not offered as evidence that utility is the key to understanding choice behavior. Rather, utility has been placed more generally in the context of these concerns. Since considerations of programs, policies, and choice behavior by others have often been based upon less evidence than yielded by this study, the hesitancy to make more concrete generalizations is quite cautious by comparison.

Programs and policies are often established on the basis of assumptions about associations, which in turn are based either on opinion and speculation rather than on research, or are influenced by studies that reveal statistically significant but weaker relationships than found between utility and behavior here. For example, some programs focus upon the treatment of stress, rebelliousness, or boredom of young people, because it is assumed these are important determinants of drug use, and that their alleviation would thereby decrease the use of drugs. In fact, these variables were seldom related to marijuana behavior in our study (Chapter 7), and when found to be correlated with behavior in other research they were typically weaker than the associations between utility and behavior in this study. (For comparisons, see the studies cited in Jessor 1979; Kandel 1978; and Lettieri 1975.) Some researchers have studied choice behavior and made substantial claims about the importance of their explanatory variables when the relationships they observed were weaker than those found in the research reported here.

It is felt that stronger relationships between causal variables and behavior than found in this study are desirable before definitive decisions are made about programs, policies, and choice behavior. However, since the strength of the relationship between utility and behavior in this study might have been reduced for the methodological reasons previously mentioned, and because others with less compelling evidence are often more liberal with their generalizations, the reader may choose to give the present findings more weight than did the researchers, when considering programs, policies, and choice behavior. And, of course, some may choose to award the findings less weight, but before doing this it is hoped that they will make careful comparisons of the findings with the evidence from other sources. In any case, without qualification, future research can be encouraged to determine whether, through improvements in measurement and other methodological aspects, the strength of the relationship between utility and behavior can be enhanced.

REFERENCES

Bentham, Jeremy. 1948. (Originally printed in 1780.) A Fragment on Government and an Introduction to the Principles of Morals and Legislation. Edited by Wilfred Harrison. Oxford: Basil Blackwell.

Fishbein, Martin, and Icek Ajzen. 1975. Belief, Attitude, Intention and Behavior: An Introduction to Theory and Research. Reading, Mass.: Addison-Wesley.

Halleck, Seymour. 1970. "The Great Drug Education Hoax." Progressive 34: 30-33.

Jessor, Richard. 1979. "Marijuana: A Review of Recent Psychosocial Research." In Handbook on Drug Abuse, edited by Robert I. Dupont, Avram Goldstein, and John O'Donnel, pp. 337-55. Washington, D.C.: Government Printing Office.

Kandel, Denise, ed. 1978. Longitudinal Research on Drug Use: Empirical Findings and Methodological Issues. New York: Wiley.

Lettieri, Dan J., ed. 1975. Predicting Adolescent Drug Abuse: A Review of Issues, Methods and Correlates, DHEW Publication No. (ADM) 76-299. Washington, D.C.: Government Printing Office.

Levy, Marvin R. 1971. "Drug Abuse Education: A Pedagogical Schizophrenia." American Journal of Pharmacy 143: 51-57.

National Institute on Drug Abuse. 1974. Alternative Pursuits for America's 3rd Century, A Resource Book on New Perceptions, Processes, and Programs—With Implications for the Prevention of Drug Abuse, DHEW Publication No. (HSM) 73-9158. Washington, D. C.: Government Printing Office.

Ungerleider, J. Thomas, and Haskell L. Bowen. 1969. "Drug Abuse and the Schools." American Journal of Psychiatry 125: 1691-97.

Vogl, A. J. 1970. "Influencing Kids Against Drugs—What Works?" Medical Economics 47: 124-34.

Wald, Patricia M., and Annette Abrams. 1972. "Drug Education." In Dealing with Drug Abuse, edited by Patricia M. Wald and Peter Barton Hutt et al. New York: Praeger.

Weimar, Robert H. 1972. "Toward a Model of Primary Prevention of Drug Abuse in Elementary Schools." British Journal of Addiction 68: 57-63.

Zanowiak, Paul. 1970. "Drug Abuse Education Programming for a Rural State—One Approach." Journal of the American Pharmaceutical Association, NS10: 566-71.

APPENDIX A
THE QUESTIONNAIRE

THE QUESTIONNAIRE

Section A of Questionnaire

From the list below, pick out the GOOD THINGS that you think
might happen to you if you used marijuana (grass, pot, reefers).
Check each THING you pick out.

___ GET HIGH (GET THRILLS OR KICKS, HAVE A GOOD TIME)
___ HAVE OTHER KIDS THINK THAT I AM COOL
___ FEEL AS IF TIME WERE PASSING SLOWER
___ HAVE MORE SELF-CONFIDENCE
___ BE ABLE TO DO THINGS BETTER
___ FEEL MORE PLEASURE (FEEL GOOD)
___ FEEL CLOSER TO OTHERS
___ ENJOY DOING THINGS WITH MY FRIENDS
___ FEEL STRONGER
___ ENJOY THE TASTE
___ UNDERSTAND MYSELF BETTER
___ ACT AGAINST MY PARENTS, OTHER ADULTS OR SOCIETY
    (TO REBEL)
___ FEEL AT HOME WITH THE GROUP
___ SEE, SMELL, TASTE, HEAR OR FEEL THINGS BETTER
___ BE LESS BORED
___ HAVE LESS PAIN
___ WORRY LESS (BE ABLE TO FORGET ABOUT PROBLEMS
    FOR A WHILE)
___ HAVE DIFFERENT OR INTERESTING THOUGHTS
___ FEEL MORE IMPORTANT OR GROWN-UP
___ SLEEP BETTER
___ FEEL HAPPIER (NOT FEEL SO "LOW," OR DOWN IN THE
    DUMPS OR DEPRESSED)
___ BE ABLE TO THINK BETTER (FOR EXAMPLE, REMEMBER
    THINGS BETTER, LEARN FASTER, HAVE BETTER CONCEN-
    TRATION, SOLVE MY PROBLEMS BETTER, GET BETTER
    GRADES)
___ BE MORE RELAXED
___ HELP ME CONTROL MY WEIGHT
___ SATISFY MY CURIOSITY (FIND OUT WHAT IT IS LIKE)
___ BE LIKED MORE BY MY FRIENDS OR HAVE MORE FRIENDS

ONLY for the THINGS YOU MARKED, answer the questions by
writing one of the following numbers beside your mark.
1 UNIMPORTANT   2   ONLY SLIGHTLY IMPORTANT
3 SOMEWHAT IMPORTANT   4   QUITE IMPORTANT
5 VERY VERY IMPORTANT

____ How important is it to you to GET HIGH (GET THRILLS OR
KICKS, HAVE A GOOD TIME) ?

____ How important is it to you for OTHER KIDS TO THINK THAT
YOU ARE COOL ?

____ How important is it to you to FEEL AS IF TIME WERE
PASSING SLOWER ?

____ How important is it to you to HAVE MORE SELF-CONFIDENCE ?

____ How important is it to you to BE ABLE TO DO THINGS BETTER ?

____ How important is it to you to FEEL MORE PLEASURE (FEEL
GOOD) ?

____ How important is it to you to FEEL CLOSER TO OTHERS ?

____ How important is it to you to ENJOY DOING THINGS WITH
YOUR FRIENDS ?

____ How important is it to you to FEEL STRONGER ?

____ How important is it to you to ENJOY THE TASTE OF SOME-
THING ?

____ How important is it to you to UNDERSTAND YOURSELF BETTER ?

____ How important is it to you to ACT AGAINST YOUR PARENTS,
OTHER ADULTS, OR SOCIETY (TO REBEL) ?

____ How important is it to you to FEEL AT HOME WITH THE GROUP ?

____ How important is it to you to SEE, SMELL, TASTE, HEAR OR
FEEL THINGS BETTER ?

____ How important is it to you to BE LESS BORED ?

____ How important is it to you to HAVE LESS PAIN ?

____ How important is it to you to WORRY LESS (BE ABLE TO
FORGET ABOUT PROBLEMS FOR A WHILE) ?

____ How important is it to you to HAVE DIFFERENT OR INTEREST-
ING THOUGHTS ?

____ How important is it to you to FEEL MORE IMPORTANT AND
GROWN-UP ?

____ How important is it to you to SLEEP BETTER ?

____ How important is it to you to FEEL HAPPIER (NOT FEEL SO
"LOW" OR DOWN IN THE DUMPS OR DEPRESSED) ?

____ How important is it to you to BE ABLE TO THINK BETTER
(FOR EXAMPLE, REMEMBER THINGS BETTER, LEARN
FASTER, HAVE BETTER CONCENTRATION, SOLVE YOUR
PROBLEMS BETTER, GET BETTER GRADES) ?

____ How important is it to you to BE MORE RELAXED ?

____ How important is it to you to CONTROL YOUR WEIGHT ?

____ How important is it to you to SATISFY YOUR CURIOSITY
(FIND OUT WHAT NEW THINGS ARE LIKE)?

____ How important is it to you to BE LIKED MORE BY YOUR
FRIENDS OR HAVE MORE FRIENDS?

ONLY for the THINGS YOU MARKED, answer the questions by
writing one of the following numbers beside your mark.
1 IMPOSSIBLE   2 NOT VERY LIKELY   3 SOMEWHAT LIKELY
4 VERY LIKELY   5 ABSOLUTELY CERTAIN

____ If you used marijuana, how LIKELY is it that you would GET
HIGH (GET THRILLS OR KICKS, HAVE A GOOD TIME)?

____ If you used marijuana, how LIKELY is it that OTHER KIDS
WOULD THINK THAT YOU WERE COOL?

____ If you used marijuana, how LIKELY is it that you would FEEL
AS IF TIME WERE PASSING SLOWER?

____ If you used marijuana, how LIKELY is it that you would HAVE
MORE SELF-CONFIDENCE?

____ If you used marijuana, how LIKELY is it that you would BE
ABLE TO DO THINGS BETTER?

____ If you used marijuana, how LIKELY is it that you would FEEL
MORE PLEASURE (FEEL GOOD)?

____ If you used marijuana, how LIKELY is it that you would FEEL
CLOSER TO OTHERS?

____ If you used marijuana, how LIKELY is it that you would ENJOY
DOING THINGS WITH YOUR FRIENDS?

____ If you used marijuana, how LIKELY is it that you would FEEL
STRONGER?

____ If you used marijuana, how LIKELY is it that you would ENJOY
THE TASTE?

____ If you used marijuana, how LIKELY is it that you would
UNDERSTAND YOURSELF BETTER?

____ If you used marijuana, how LIKELY is it that you would ACT
AGAINST YOUR PARENTS, OTHER ADULTS, OR SOCIETY
(TO REBEL)?

____ If you used marijuana, how LIKELY is it that you would FEEL
AT HOME WITH THE GROUP?

____ If you used marijuana, how LIKELY is it that you would SEE,
SMELL, TASTE, HEAR OR FEEL THINGS BETTER?

____ If you used marijuana, how LIKELY is it that you would BE
LESS BORED?

____ If you used marijuana, how LIKELY is it that you would HAVE
LESS PAIN?

____ If you used marijuana, how LIKELY is it that you would WORRY
LESS (BE ABLE TO FORGET ABOUT PROBLEMS FOR A
WHILE)?

___ If you used marijuana, how LIKELY is it that you would HAVE DIFFERENT OR INTERESTING THOUGHTS?

___ If you used marijuana, how LIKELY is it that you would FEEL MORE IMPORTANT OR GROWN-UP?

___ If you used marijuana, how LIKELY is it that you would SLEEP BETTER?

___ If you used marijuana, how LIKELY is it that you would FEEL HAPPIER (NOT FEEL SO "LOW," OR DOWN IN THE DUMPS OR DEPRESSED)?

___ If you used marijuana, how LIKELY is it that you would BE ABLE TO THINK BETTER (FOR EXAMPLE, REMEMBER THINGS BETTER, LEARN FASTER, HAVE BETTER CON- CENTRATION, SOLVE YOUR PROBLEMS BETTER, GET BETTER GRADES)?

___ If you used marijuana, how LIKELY is it that you would BE MORE RELAXED?

___ If you used marijuana, how LIKELY is it that it would HELP YOU CONTROL YOUR WEIGHT?

___ If you used marijuana, how LIKELY is it that it would SATISFY YOUR CURIOSITY (FIND OUT WHAT IT IS LIKE)?

___ If you used marijuana, how LIKELY is it that you would BE LIKED MORE BY YOUR FRIENDS OR HAVE MORE FRIENDS?

Section B of Questionnaire

From the list below, pick out the BAD THINGS that you think might happen to you if you used marijuana (grass, pot, reefers). Check each THING you pick out.

___ BE ARRESTED BY THE POLICE

___ BE A BAD EXAMPLE FOR OTHERS

___ DO STRANGE OR DANGEROUS THINGS, LOSE CONTROL OVER MYSELF

___ NOT LIVE AS LONG

___ FEEL LIKE I AM GOING CRAZY (HAVE SCARY OR STRANGE THOUGHTS)

___ BE LESS UNDERSTANDING OF MYSELF

___ NOT BE ABLE TO THINK AS WELL (FORGET THINGS MORE, LEARN SLOWER, BE UNABLE TO CONCENTRATE, BE LESS CREATIVE)

___ BECOME MORE NERVOUS

___ GET INTO TROUBLE WITH PARENTS

___ CAUSE ACCIDENTS

___ GO ON TO MORE HARMFUL DRUGS

___ BE SADDER (FEEL LOW OR DOWN)
___ LOSE INTEREST IN THINGS
___ NOT BE ABLE TO DO THINGS SUCH AS RUNNING OR WALKING
AS WELL
___ GO TO JAIL
___ FEEL AS IF TIME WERE PASSING SLOWER
___ BE LIKED LESS BY FRIENDS OR HAVE FEWER FRIENDS
___ FEEL GUILTY BECAUSE IT IS AGAINST THE LAW, OR BE-
CAUSE IT IS AGAINST MY RELIGION, OR BECAUSE IT IS
AGAINST MY MORALS
___ FEEL BAD (GET SICK, HURT, DIZZY, PAINFUL OR WEAK)
___ GET INTO TROUBLE WITH THE TEACHER OR PRINCIPAL
___ GET INTO TROUBLE WITH PEOPLE WHO SELL DRUGS
___ HAVE TO SPEND TOO MUCH MONEY
___ GET INTO TROUBLE WITH THE POLICE
___ HARM MY BODY FOREVER
___ LOSE RESPECT FOR MYSELF
___ DISLIKE THE TASTE
___ NOT BE ABLE TO STOP USING DRUGS (BECOME "HOOKED")
___ DIE FROM AN OVERDOSE (DIE FROM TAKING TOO MUCH)

ONLY for the THINGS YOU MARKED, answer the questions by writing one of the following numbers beside your mark
1 UNIMPORTANT   2 ONLY SLIGHTLY IMPORTANT
3 SOMEWHAT IMPORTANT   4 QUITE IMPORTANT
5 VERY VERY IMPORTANT

___ How important is it to you NOT TO BE ARRESTED BY THE
POLICE ?
___ How important is it to you NOT TO BE A BAD EXAMPLE FOR
OTHERS?
___ How important is it to you NOT TO DO STRANGE OR DANGEROUS
THINGS, NOT LOSE CONTROL OVER YOURSELF ?
___ How important is it to you TO LIVE AS LONG AS POSSIBLE ?
___ How important is it to you NOT TO FEEL LIKE YOU ARE
GOING CRAZY (NOT HAVE SCARY OR STRANGE THOUGHTS) ?
___ How important is it to you TO BE UNDERSTANDING OF
YOURSELF ?
___ How important is it to you TO BE ABLE TO THINK AS WELL AS
YOU DO NOW (NOT FORGET THINGS MORE, NOT LEARN
SLOWER, NOT BE UNABLE TO CONCENTRATE, NOT BE
LESS CREATIVE) ?
___ How important is it to you NOT TO BECOME MORE NERVOUS?
___ How important is it to you NOT TO GET INTO TROUBLE WITH
PARENTS?

___ How important is it to you NOT TO CAUSE ACCIDENTS?

___ How important is it to you NOT TO GO ON TO MORE HARMFUL DRUGS?

___ How important is it to you NOT TO BE SADDER (NOT FEEL LOW OR DOWN)?

___ How important is it to you NOT TO LOSE INTEREST IN THINGS?

___ How important is it to you to BE ABLE TO DO THINGS SUCH AS RUNNING OR WALKING AS WELL AS YOU DO NOW?

___ How important is it to you NOT TO GO TO JAIL?

___ How important is it to you NOT TO FEEL AS IF TIME WERE PASSING SLOWER?

___ How important is it to you NOT TO BE LIKED LESS BY FRIENDS OR NOT TO HAVE FEWER FRIENDS?

___ How important is it to you NOT TO FEEL GUILTY BECAUSE SOMETHING YOU DO IS AGAINST THE LAW OR AGAINST YOUR RELIGION OR AGAINST YOUR MORALS?

___ How important is it to you NOT TO FEEL BAD (NOT TO GET SICK, HURT, DIZZY, PAINFUL, OR WEAK)?

___ How important is it to you NOT TO GET INTO TROUBLE WITH THE TEACHER OR PRINCIPAL?

___ How important is it to you NOT TO GET INTO TROUBLE WITH PEOPLE WHO SELL DRUGS?

___ How important is it to you NOT TO HAVE TO SPEND TOO MUCH MONEY?

___ How important is it to you NOT TO GET INTO TROUBLE WITH THE POLICE?

___ How important is it to you NOT TO HARM YOUR BODY FOR-EVER?

___ How important is it to you NOT TO LOSE RESPECT FOR YOUR-SELF?

___ How important is it to you NOT TO DISLIKE HOW SOMETHING TASTES?

___ How important is it to you TO BE ABLE TO STOP USING DRUGS (NOT TO BE HOOKED)?

___ How important is it to you NOT TO DIE FROM AN OVERDOSE (NOT TO DIE FROM TAKING TOO MUCH OF SOMETHING)?

ONLY for the THINGS YOU MARKED, answer the questions by writing one of the following numbers beside your mark
1 IMPOSSIBLE   2 NOT VERY LIKELY   3 SOMEWHAT LIKELY
4 VERY LIKELY   5 ABSOLUTELY CERTAIN

___ If you used marijuana, how LIKELY is it that you would be ARRESTED BY THE POLICE?

___ If you used marijuana, how LIKELY is it that you would BE A BAD EXAMPLE FOR OTHERS?

___ If you used marijuana, how LIKELY is it that you would DO STRANGE OR DANGEROUS THINGS, LOSE CONTROL OVER YOURSELF?

___ If you used marijuana, how LIKELY is it that you would NOT LIVE AS LONG?

___ If you used marijuana, how LIKELY is it that you would FEEL LIKE YOU WERE GOING CRAZY (HAVE SCARY OR STRANGE THOUGHTS)?

___ If you used marijuana, how LIKELY is it that you would BE LESS UNDERSTANDING OF YOURSELF?

___ If you used marijuana, how LIKELY is it that you would NOT BE ABLE TO THINK AS WELL (FORGET THINGS MORE, LEARN SLOWER, BE UNABLE TO CONCENTRATE, BE LESS CREATIVE)?

___ If you used marijuana, how LIKELY is it that you would BECOME MORE NERVOUS?

___ If you used marijuana, how LIKELY is it that you would GET INTO TROUBLE WITH PARENTS?

___ If you used marijuana, how LIKELY is it that you would CAUSE ACCIDENTS?

___ If you used marijuana, how LIKELY is it that you would GO ON TO MORE HARMFUL DRUGS?

___ If you used marijuana, how LIKELY is it that you would BE SADDER (FEEL LOW OR DOWN)?

___ If you used marijuana, how LIKELY is it that you would LOSE INTEREST IN THINGS?

___ If you used marijuana, how LIKELY is it that you would NOT BE ABLE TO DO THINGS SUCH AS RUNNING OR WALKING AS WELL?

___ If you used marijuana, how LIKELY is it that you would GO TO JAIL?

___ If you used marijuana, how LIKELY is it that you would FEEL AS IF TIME WERE PASSING SLOWER?

___ If you used marijuana, how LIKELY is it that you would BE LIKED LESS BY FRIENDS OR HAVE FEWER FRIENDS?

___ If you used marijuana, how LIKELY is it that you would FEEL GUILTY BECAUSE IT IS AGAINST THE LAW, OR BECAUSE IT IS AGAINST YOUR RELIGION, OR BECAUSE IT IS AGAINST YOUR MORALS?

___ If you used marijuana, how LIKELY is it that you would FEEL BAD (GET SICK, HURT, DIZZY, PAINFUL OR WEAK)?

___ If you used marijuana, how LIKELY is it that you would GET INTO TROUBLE WITH THE TEACHER OR PRINCIPAL?

___ If you used marijuana, how LIKELY is it that you would GET INTO TROUBLE WITH PEOPLE WHO SELL DRUGS?

___ If you used marijuana, how LIKELY is it that you would HAVE
TO SPEND TOO MUCH MONEY?

___ If you used marijuana, how LIKELY is it that you would GET
INTO TROUBLE WITH THE POLICE?

___ If you used marijuana, how LIKELY is it that you would HARM
YOUR BODY FOREVER?

___ If you used marijuana, how LIKELY is it that you would LOSE
RESPECT FOR YOURSELF?

___ If you used marijuana, how LIKELY is it that you would DISLIKE
THE TASTE?

___ If you used marijuana, how LIKELY is it that you would NOT BE
ABLE TO STOP USING DRUGS (BECOME "HOOKED")?

___ If you used marijuana, how LIKELY is it that you would DIE
FROM AN OVERDOSE (DIE FROM TAKING TOO MUCH)?

Section C of Questionnaire

The next questions are about marijuana too. PLEASE CHECK ONLY
ONE ANSWER FOR EACH QUESTION.

1. Think of all the good and bad things about marijuana. If you
   used marijuana, do you think it would do you:
   1 ___ more good than harm, or
   2 ___ more harm than good?
2. Think of all the good and bad things that might happen to you if
   you used marijuana: which are more important to you?
   1 ___ The good things are more important than the bad things.
   2 ___ The bad things are more important than the good things.
   3 ___ The good and bad things are about equally important.
3. Suppose you wanted to get some marijuana. How easy or hard
   would it be for you to get?
   1 ___ Very easy
   2 ___ Somewhat easy
   3 ___ Somewhat hard
   4 ___ Very hard
4. Have you ever been taught about marijuana or other drugs in
   any classes at school?
   1 ___ Yes
   2 ___ No
5. How often do you and one or both of your two best friends talk
   about marijuana?
   1 ___ Often
   2 ___ Sometimes
   3 ___ Seldom
   4 ___ Never

6. How many of your two best friends have used marijuana?
   1 ___ Neither of my two best friends have used marijuana.
   2 ___ One of my two best friends has used marijuana.
   3 ___ Both of my two best friends have used marijuana.
   4 ___ I don't know.

7. How LIKELY do you think it is that you will use marijuana at least once during the next nine months?
   1 ___ Impossible (I am sure I will never use marijuana during the next nine months.)
   2 ___ Not very likely
   3 ___ Somewhat likely
   4 ___ Very likely
   5 ___ Absolutely certain (I am sure I will use marijuana at least once during the next nine months.)

8. How LIKELY do you think it is that you will use marijuana at least once during the next ten years?
   1 ___ Impossible (I am sure I will never use marijuana during the next ten years.)
   2 ___ Not very likely
   3 ___ Somewhat likely
   4 ___ Very likely
   5 ___ Absolutely certain (I am sure I will use marijuana at least once during the next ten years.)

9. How often have you used marijuana?
   1 ___ Never used marijuana
   2 ___ 1-2 times
   3 ___ 3-4 times
   4 ___ 5-9 times
   5 ___ 10-39 times
   6 ___ 40 or more times

10. How old were you when you first used marijuana?
    1 ___ Never used marijuana
    2 ___ 10 years old or younger
    3 ___ 11 years old
    4 ___ 12 years old
    5 ___ 13 years old
    6 ___ 14 years old
    7 ___ 15 years old or older

11. During what time of the year did you first use marijuana?
    1 ___ Never used marijuana
    2 ___ Spring (March, April, May)
    3 ___ Summer (June, July, August)
    4 ___ Fall (September, October, November)
    5 ___ Winter (December, January, February)

12. How long has it been since you last used marijuana?
    1 ___ Never used marijuana
    2 ___ Today
    3 ___ 1-7 days ago
    4 ___ 8-14 days ago
    5 ___ 15-30 days ago
    6 ___ 31-90 days ago
    7 ___ 91-180 days ago
    8 ___ 181-365 days ago
    9 ___ over 365 days ago

13. How many days have you used marijuana during the past 30 days?
    1 ___ No days
    2 ___ One day
    3 ___ 2-3 days
    4 ___ 4-7 days
    5 ___ 8-11 days
    6 ___ More than 11 days

14. With whom do you usually use marijuana?
    1 ___ Never used marijuana
    2 ___ Alone
    3 ___ Others my age
    4 ___ Others much younger than me
    5 ___ Others much older than me

15. How did you get marijuana the first time you used it?
    1 ___ Never used marijuana
    2 ___ It was given to me for free
    3 ___ I gave money for it
    4 ___ I got it some other way

16. Who gave you marijuana the first time you used it?
    1 ___ Never used marijuana
    2 ___ A friend
    3 ___ A relative
    4 ___ Someone other than a friend or relative

17. Where were you the first time you used marijuana?
    1 ___ Never used marijuana
    2 ___ At home
    3 ___ At school
    4 ___ Some place other than home or school

18. Who were you with the first time you used marijuana?
    1 ___ Never used marijuana
    2 ___ No one (I was alone)
    3 ___ With others my age who were friends
    4 ___ With others my age who were not my friends
    5 ___ With others not my age

The next questions ask about drugs other than marijuana. CHECK
ONLY ONE ANSWER FOR EACH QUESTION.

19. Have you ever tried BEER without your parents knowing it?
    1 ___ Yes
    2 ___ No
20. Have you ever tried WINE without your parents knowing it?
    1 ___ Yes
    2 ___ No
21. Have you ever tried HARD LIQUOR (bourbon, gin, rum,
    whiskey, scotch, or vodka, but not including beer or wine)
    without your parents knowing it?
    1 ___ Yes
    2 ___ No
22. Have you ever smoked a CIGARETTE?
    1 ___ Yes
    2 ___ No
23. Have you ever taken LSD ("acid," "trips")?
    1 ___ Yes
    2 ___ No
24. Have you ever taken PSYCHEDELIC DRUGS other than LSD,
    such as, DMT, STP, psilocybin, mescaline, peyote?
    1 ___ Yes
    2 ___ No
25. Have you ever taken METHEDRINE ("meth," "speed")?
    1 ___ Yes
    2 ___ No
26. Have you ever taken "UPS" - OTHER AMPHETAMINES ("pep
    pills," "diet pills," "bennies," "dexies") dexedrine, benzedrine,
    dexampyl?
    1 ___ Yes
    2 ___ No
27. Have you ever taken "DOWNS" - BARBITURATES ("goofballs,"
    "Blues," "yellows," "reds") seconal, nembutal, tuinal,
    phenobarbital?
    1 ___ Yes
    2 ___ No
28. Have you ever taken TRANQUILIZERS (equanil, miltown,
    librium, valium, thorazine) without your parents knowing it?
    1 ___ Yes
    2 ___ No
29. Have you ever taken COCAINE?
    1 ___ Yes
    2 ___ No

30. Have you ever taken HEROIN?
   1 ___ Yes
   2 ___ No
31. Have you ever taken OTHER NARCOTICS, OPIATES (opium, morphine, dolophine, methadone, demerol, darvon)?
   1 ___ Yes
   2 ___ No
32. Have you ever taken COUGH SYRUP when you didn't have a cough or cold?
   1 ___ Yes
   2 ___ No
33. Have you ever sniffed INHALANTS (glue, freon, carbona) except when you were using it to glue something?
   1 ___ Yes
   2 ___ No
34. Have you ever used ADRENOCHROMES ("wagon wheels")?
   1 ___ Yes
   2 ___ No

The rest of the questions are not about marijuana or other drugs. These questions are about you, how you feel, and what you think about things in general. CHECK ONLY ONE ANSWER FOR EACH QUESTION.

35. How often do you think about what your life will be like one year from today?
   1 ___ Very often
   2 ___ Sometimes
   3 ___ Not very often
   4 ___ Never
36. How often do you think about what your life will be like ten years from today?
   1 ___ Very often
   2 ___ Sometimes
   3 ___ Not very often
   4 ___ Never
37. If someone gave you $50.00 tomorrow and you didn't have anything you needed to spend it on would you:
   1 ___ Spend it right away anyway
   2 ___ Save it until you needed something
38. If you could pick one of the choices below, which one would you pick?
   1 ___ Fifty dollars now
   2 ___ Fifty-five dollars tomorrow
   3 ___ Seventy dollars two weeks from today
   4 ___ One hundred dollars two months from today
   5 ___ Four hundred dollars one year from today

39. How often do you and one or both of your two best friends get together at a place other than school?
    1 ___ Every day
    2 ___ Several times a week
    3 ___ About once a week
    4 ___ Less than once a week

40. How many days out of the past 30 have you gone out on a date with a person of the opposite sex?
    1 ___ 0 days
    2 ___ 1 day
    3 ___ 2-3 days
    4 ___ 4-7 days
    5 ___ 8-11 days
    6 ___ more than 11 days

41. How many days out of the past 30 have you watched TV alone without having friends over?
    1 ___ 0 days
    2 ___ 1 day
    3 ___ 2-3 days
    4 ___ 4-7 days
    5 ___ 8-11 days
    6 ___ more than 11 days

42. How many days out of the past 30 have you stayed at home and done something by yourself without having friends over?
    1 ___ 0 days
    2 ___ 1 day
    3 ___ 2-3 days
    4 ___ 4-7 days
    5 ___ 8-11 days
    6 ___ more than 11 days

43. How many days out of the past 30 have you read some of a book other than a school book?
    1 ___ 0 days
    2 ___ 1 day
    3 ___ 2-3 days
    4 ___ 4-7 days
    5 ___ 8-11 days
    6 ___ more than 11 days

44. How many days out of the past 30 have you gone to a friend's house?
    1 ___ 0 days
    2 ___ 1 day
    3 ___ 2-3 days
    4 ___ 4-7 days
    5 ___ 8-11 days
    6 ___ more than 11 days

45. How many days out of the past 30 have you gone out with friends?
    1 ___ 0 days
    2 ___ 1 day
    3 ___ 2-3 days
    4 ___ 4-7 days
    5 ___ 8-11 days
    6 ___ more than 11 days
46. How many days out of the past 30 have you participated in an activity such as sports, clubs, music?
    1 ___ 0 days
    2 ___ 1 day
    3 ___ 2-3 days
    4 ___ 4-7 days
    5 ___ 8-11 days
    6 ___ more than 11 days
47. How many days out of the past 30 have you gone out and hung around with a group of friends?
    1 ___ 0 days
    2 ___ 1 day
    3 ___ 2-3 days
    4 ___ 4-7 days
    5 ___ 8-11 days
    6 ___ more than 11 days
48. If your parents objected to one of your friends what would you do?
    1 ___ Stop seeing your friend
    2 ___ See your friend less
    3 ___ Continue to see your friend as usual
49. Whose opinion would you respect more when you have a problem—your parents' opinion or your best friends' opinion?
    1 ___ Parents' opinion much more
    2 ___ Parents' opinion a little more
    3 ___ Parents' opinion and best friends' opinion about equally
    4 ___ Best friends' opinion a little more
    5 ___ Best friends' opinion much more
50. Do you try to follow all the rules made by parents, the school, and all laws?
    1 ___ Yes
    2 ___ No
51. Do you sometimes break a rule or law if you disagree with it and think you will not get caught?
    1 ___ Yes
    2 ___ No
52. Do you sometimes break a rule or law if you disagree with it just to prove a point?
    1 ___ Yes
    2 ___ No

53. Do you often break rules or laws just for the sake of breaking them?
    1 ___ Yes
    2 ___ No
54. I am bored most of the time I am in school.
    1 ___ Agree completely
    2 ___ Agree somewhat
    3 ___ Disagree somewhat
    4 ___ Disagree completely
55. I am often bored after school and on weekends.
    1 ___ Agree completely
    2 ___ Agree somewhat
    3 ___ Disagree somewhat
    4 ___ Disagree completely
56. Summers are usually boring.
    1 ___ Agree completely
    2 ___ Agree somewhat
    3 ___ Disagree somewhat
    4 ___ Disagree completely
57. I have many activities I can look forward to doing.
    1 ___ Agree completely
    2 ___ Agree somewhat
    3 ___ Disagree somewhat
    4 ___ Disagree completely
58. Life is always interesting.
    1 ___ Agree completely
    2 ___ Agree somewhat
    3 ___ Disagree somewhat
    4 ___ Disagree completely
59. How important to you is discovering new ways to experience things?
    1 ___ Very important
    2 ___ Somewhat important
    3 ___ Only slightly important
    4 ___ Not important
60. How often do you wonder what it would be like to do something you have never done before?
    1 ___ Very often
    2 ___ Sometimes
    3 ___ Seldom
    4 ___ Never
61. In the past 30 days, how many times have you done something just to see what it would be like?
    1 ___ More than 10 times
    2 ___ 5-9 times

3 ___ 3 or 4 times
4 ___ 1 or 2 times
5 ___ 0 times

62. How much do you want to go to college?
1 ___ Very much
2 ___ Somewhat
3 ___ Not very much
4 ___ Not at all

63. How likely do you think it is that you will go to college?
1 ___ Impossible (I am sure I will not go to college)
2 ___ Not very likely
3 ___ Somewhat likely
4 ___ Very likely
5 ___ Absolutely certain (I am sure I will go to college)

64. How close do you feel to your father?
1 ___ Extremely close
2 ___ Quite close
3 ___ Moderately close
4 ___ Not particularly close
5 ___ Not at all close
6 ___ No father

65. How close do you feel to your mother?
1 ___ Extremely close
2 ___ Quite close
3 ___ Moderately close
4 ___ Not particularly close
5 ___ Not at all close
6 ___ No mother

Some parents have rules for their children, while others don't.

66. Do you usually have to be home at a certain time on weekend nights?
1 ___ Yes
2 ___ No

67. Would your parents let you go out on a date with a person of the opposite sex?
1 ___ Yes
2 ___ No

68. Do your parents let you go around with any people your age that you want to?
1 ___ Yes
2 ___ No

69. Do your parents tell you what clothes you can wear?
1 ___ Yes
2 ___ No

70. Do your parents have you go to bed about the same time on school nights?
    1 ___ Yes
    2 ___ No
71. In general, are your parents:
    1 ___ Strict about what you can and can't do, or
    2 ___ do they let you do what you want to do most of the time?
72. During the past year, how much have you been bothered or troubled by feeling too tired to do things?
    1 ___ Much
    2 ___ Somewhat
    3 ___ Not at all
73. During the past year, how much have you been bothered or troubled by having a hard time going to sleep or staying asleep?
    1 ___ Much
    2 ___ Somewhat
    3 ___ Not at all
74. During the past year, how much have you been bothered or troubled by feeling unhappy, sad or depressed?
    1 ___ Much
    2 ___ Somewhat
    3 ___ Not at all
75. During the past year, how much have you been bothered or troubled by feeling hopeless about the future?
    1 ___ Much
    2 ___ Somewhat
    3 ___ Not at all
76. During the past year, how much have you been bothered or troubled by feeling nervous or tense?
    1 ___ Much
    2 ___ Somewhat
    3 ___ Not at all
77. During the past year, how much have you been bothered or troubled by daydreaming?
    1 ___ Much
    2 ___ Somewhat
    3 ___ Not at all
78. During the past year, how much have you been bothered or troubled by worrying too much about things?
    1 ___ Much
    2 ___ Somewhat
    3 ___ Not at all
79. How important would you say religion is in your life?
    1 ___ Very important
    2 ___ Somewhat important

80. How often do you attend religious services?
    1 ___ Once a week or more
    2 ___ A few times a month
    3 ___ Several times a year
    4 ___ Rarely if ever
81. What is your sex?
    1 ___ Female
    2 ___ Male
82. What is your race?
    1 ___ Black
    2 ___ White
    3 ___ Other
83. How old are you?
    1 ___ 10 or younger
    2 ___ 11
    3 ___ 12
    4 ___ 13
    5 ___ 14
    6 ___ 15
    7 ___ 16 or older
84. How far in school did your mother go? (Mark the highest level completed.)
    1 ___ Grade school or less
    2 ___ Some high school but did not graduate
    3 ___ Graduated from high school
    4 ___ Technical or business school after high school
    5 ___ Some college but less than four years
    6 ___ Graduated from four year college
    7 ___ Attended graduate or professional school
    8 ___ Don't know
85. How far in school did your father go? (Mark the highest level completed.)
    1 ___ Grade school or less
    2 ___ Some high school but did not graduate
    3 ___ Graduated from high school
    4 ___ Technical or business school after high school
    5 ___ Some college but less than four years
    6 ___ Graduated from four year college
    7 ___ Attended graduate or professional school
    8 ___ Don't know

READ THE FOLLOWING PARAGRAPH AND ANSWER THE THREE
QUESTIONS ABOUT IT. PLEASE CHECK ONLY ONE ANSWER FOR
EACH QUESTION.

"I know you are in there," said the sheriff. "You have five
seconds to come out."

"Come get me!" shouted the robber from inside the house.

The sheriff began to count. "One. Two. Three." Suddenly,
the robber walked out with his hands up.

86. Where was the robber?
   1 ___ Inside the house
   2 ___ By the river
   3 ___ In the bushes
   4 ___ On his horse
   5 ___ In the barn
87. How long did the sheriff give him to come out?
   1 ___ Five seconds
   2 ___ One minute
   3 ___ Five minutes
   4 ___ Ten minutes
   5 ___ An hour
88. What did the robber do?
   1 ___ He ran out shooting both guns
   2 ___ He tried to escape and was shot down
   3 ___ He walked out with his hands up
   4 ___ He sneaked out and got away
   5 ___ He didn't come out, so the sheriff had to go in and
         get him

When you finish go back over Section C. Make sure you have
answered all the questions, and have marked only one answer for
each. Then, please remain quietly in your seat until the session
is over.

THANKS FOR BEING IN THE STUDY

APPENDIX B
VISUAL AID USED AS PART OF INSTRUCTIONS FOR COMPILING SECTIONS A AND B OF THE QUESTIONNAIRE

VISUAL AID USED AS PART OF INSTRUCTIONS FOR COMPLETING
SECTIONS A AND B OF QUESTIONNAIRE .

FROM THE LIST BELOW, PICK OUT BAD THINGS YOU THINK MIGHT HAPPEN TO YOU IF YOU DID
NOT CARRY AN UMBRELLA NEXT WEEK.   CHECK EACH THING YOU PICK OUT.

—— GET WET.

—— RUIN MY CLOTHES.

—— FAIL A TEST.

—— CATCH A COLD.

YOU HAVE FINISHED THIS PAGE WHEN THERE IS A MARK BESIDE EACH THING THAT YOU THINK
MIGHT HAPPEN TO YOU IF YOU DID NOT CARRY AN UMBRELLA NEXT WEEK.

ONLY FOR THE THINGS YOU MARKED, ANSWER THE QUESTIONS BY WRITING ONE OF THE
FOLLOWING NUMBERS BESIDE YOUR MARK. (1) IMPOSSIBLE (2) NOT VERY LIKELY
(3) SOMEWHAT LIKELY (4) VERY LIKELY (5) ABSOLUTELY CERTAIN

___ IF YOU DID NOT CARRY AN UMBRELLA NEXT WEEK, HOW LIKELY IS IT THAT YOU
WOULD GET WET ?

___ IF YOU DID NOT CARRY AN UMBRELLA NEXT WEEK, HOW LIKELY IS IT THAT YOU
WOULD RUIN YOUR CLOTHES ?

___ IF YOU DID NOT CARRY AN UMBRELLA NEXT WEEK, HOW LIKELY IS IT THAT YOU
WOULD FAIL A TEST ?

___ IF YOU DID NOT CARRY AN UMBRELLA NEXT WEEK, HOW LIKELY IS IT THAT YOU
WOULD CATCH A COLD ?

YOU HAVE FINISHED THIS PAGE WHEN THERE IS A 1, 2, 3, 4, OR 5, BESIDE EACH THING
YOU MARKED.

ONLY FOR THE THINGS YOU MARKED, ANSWER THE QUESTIONS BY WRITING ONE OF THE FOLLOWING NUMBERS BESIDE YOUR MARK. (1) UNIMPORTANT (2) ONLY SLIGHTLY IMPORTANT (3) SOMEWHAT IMPORTANT (4) QUITE IMPORTANT (5) VERY, VERY IMPORTANT

____ HOW IMPORTANT IS IT TO YOU NOT TO GET WET ?

____ HOW IMPORTANT IS IT TO YOU NOT TO RUIN YOUR CLOTHES ?

____ HOW IMPORTANT IS IT TO YOU NOT TO FAIL A TEST ?

____ HOW IMPORTANT IS IT TO YOU NOT TO CATCH A COLD ?

YOU HAVE FINISHED THIS PAGE WHEN THERE IS A 1, 2, 3, 4, OR 5 BESIDE EACH THING YOU MARKED.

APPENDIX C
INFORMED CONSENT LETTER
FOR ROUND 1

INFORMED CONSENT LETTER FOR ROUND 1

THE UNIVERSITY OF NORTH CAROLINA
AT
CHAPEL HILL
22514

School of Public Health   Telephone
Department of Maternal   Area 919 966-2017
    and Child Health   February 20, 1976

Dear Parent:

    I am writing to ask your cooperation in a study to be conducted
at the school of your seventh grader. Your cooperation and child's
participation will make possible a study which could help many
parents and children in the future.

    There is a great need for correct information that would help
prevent drug abuse, and that can be obtained only through careful
study. The purpose of the study is to determine why some young
people begin using drugs and others do not.

    The Department of Maternal and Child Health of the University
of North Carolina's School of Public Health, in collaboration with the
Wake County Schools and other school systems in North Carolina, is
conducting a study of seventh graders which will help understanding
of drug use. Some facts about the study are listed below.

1.   All seventh graders at the school are eligible to
    participate in the study, regardless of how much
    or how little they might know about drugs.

2.   No drugs will be given as part of the study. Ques-
    tionnaires to be completed by each seventh grader
    will be administered to identify attitudes, opinions,
    and behavior. If you wish to examine our question-
    naires, copies are on file in the Office of the
    Principal.

3.　The questionnaire will be administered during two periods at school in March, April, or May. Your child will be asked to complete one or perhaps two more questionnaires at school sometime during the next twelve (12) months. No additional time will be required from you or your child. The school has determined this study will not affect school work.

4.　All information given by your child will be kept completely confidential. No questionnaire will be made available to persons other than members of our small research staff, and they will not know the names of children who completed them. We will not single out individuals, but present results in tabular form for the entire school.

5.　Your child's participation is entirely voluntary. If you or your child choose to not participate, or begin the study and decide against continuing, we will respect that decision fully. That decision will not affect you or your child in any way.

6.　If you are not against your child's participation, we will explain the study fully to your child at school, and he or she will also have the opportunity to decide whether to participate.

Please sign your name on ONE of the lines below.

A.　I _____ WANT my
　　(Sign Here if you WANT your child in the study)
child in the study.

My child's name is: _____
Please return this letter in the enclosed envelope by March 5, 1976.

B.　I _____ DO
　　(Sign Here Only if you DON'T want your child in the study)
NOT WANT my child in the study.

My child's name is: _____
Please return this letter in the enclosed envelope by March 5, 1976.

C. <u>If you do not return this letter to us by March 5, 1976,</u> we
will assume you are not against your child being in the study.
We will explain the study fully to your child at school, and
give him or her the opportunity to decide whether to be in the
study.

We hope you agree this is a worthwhile and much needed study.
If you have any questions, please feel free to call me collect at
966-2017 in Chapel Hill. Thank you very much for your consideration.

Cordially,

Karl E. Bauman, Ph.D.
Study Director

KEB/bj

Enclosure

APPENDIX D
INFORMATION FORM FOR ROUND 1

INFORMATION FORM FOR ROUND 1

INFORMATION FORM

Study of Drug Use Among Youth
Department of Maternal and Child Health
School of Public Health
University of North Carolina at Chapel Hill
Chapel Hill, North Carolina 27514

KARL E. BAUMAN, STUDY DIRECTOR

1. <u>Purpose</u>. The purpose of this study is to improve understand-
    ing of drug behavior. We believe it can help many young
    people.

2. <u>Procedures</u>. We hope you will be in the study by completing
    questionnaires today, and one or two more during the next
    12 months.

3. <u>NO ONE will know the answers YOU give</u>. To know your
    change in attitudes and behavior, we must be able to put the
    questionnaire you complete today with those we ask you to
    complete later. We will do this in a way that NO ONE will be
    able to see the information you give and know it was you who
    gave it.
        We will ask you to print your name on a pink slip that
    has the same number as your questionnaire. ALL pink slips
    will be given to one person who will <u>never</u> show them to any-
    one else. That person will <u>never</u> see the information from
    your questionnaire.
        We will do this each time we ask you to complete ques-
    tionnaires. The person with the pink slips will then give us
    the numbers from the different questionnaires you complete,
    but not your name. People with the information from the
    questionnaires will have only the numbers, and <u>never</u> your
    name.
        In this way, NO ONE will be able to look at the informa-
    tion you give us and know it was you who gave it. We are doing
    this so that you will feel completely free to tell us what you
    really think, feel, and do.

165

4. <u>Being in the study is voluntary</u>. You should feel completely free to not be in the study if you don't want to. If you decide to begin now, you should feel free to stop at any time. We will respect your decision and this will not affect you in any way.

5. <u>More information about the study</u>. If you have questions, please ask the person giving the questionnaire. Also, please feel free to write, call, or visit our office in Chapel Hill at any time.

6. <u>Examine the questionnaire</u>. Please examine the questionnaire now and feel free to ask any questions about it you wish.

7. <u>Do you need more information</u>? If you have not received enough information to make a decision about whether you want to be in the study, please ask for more information from the person giving the questionnaire.

I WANT TO BE IN THE STUDY

If you have enough information to make a decision about whether you want to be in the study, and if you want to be in the study, please <u>sign</u> your name here.

_____

NAME

I DON'T WANT TO BE IN THE STUDY

If you have enough information to make a decision about whether you want to be in the study, and if you don't want to be in the study, please take your materials to the person at the back of the room. Or, if you wish, you can stay in your seat until others leave.

THANK YOU VERY MUCH FOR YOUR TIME

KARL E. BAUMAN
STUDY DIRECTOR

APPENDIX E
INFORMED CONSENT LETTER
FOR ROUND 2

THE UNIVERSITY OF NORTH CAROLINA
AT
CHAPEL HILL

School of Public Health
Department of Maternal
and Child Health

The University of North Carolina
at Chapel Hill
Rosenau Hall 201 H
Chapel Hill, N. C. 27514

February, 1977

Dear Parent or Guardian:

We have been conducting a study to determine why some young people begin using abusive drugs and others do not because we believe that this information will help prevent use of such drugs. This study is being conducted in collaboration with the Wake County Schools.

In March or April of last year your child was one of 1,686 seventh graders who completed a questionnaire at a Wake County school. We need to have these children complete another questionnaire to know if any changes have occurred since then. In order to analyze the data already collected from the children, and to be able to have them complete another questionnaire, it is necessary to have the written permission of their parents or guardians. Before asking you to consider giving this permission for your child I want you to know more about the study.

1.   Children are eligible to be in the study regardless of how much or how little they might know about drugs.

2.   The questionnaires ask about attitudes, opinions, and behavior. Included are questions about use or nonuse of such drugs as marijuana, alcohol, and heroin. If you wish to examine our questionnaire, copies are on file in the Office of the Principal.

3.   No drugs are given as part of the study, and no information is given on how or where they are obtained.

4. The questionnaires will be administered again during two periods at your child's school in the Spring or Fall of this year. No additional time will be required of you or your child. The school has determined this study will not affect schoolwork.

5. All information given by your child will be kept completely confidential. No questionnaire will be made available to persons other than members of our small research staff, and they will not know the names of children who completed them. We will not single out individuals, but present results in tabular form for the entire school.

6. Your child's participation is entirely voluntary. If you and your child choose to not participate, or begin the study and decide against continuing, we will respect that decision fully. That decision will not affect you and your child in any way.

7. If you permit your child to be in the study, we will explain the study fully to your child at school, and he or she will also have the opportunity to decide whether to participate.

In order for us to be able to analyze the information from the questionnaire your child completed last March or April, and for your child to complete a second questionnaire, we need to have your signature on <u>both</u> statements A and B below.

A. I _____ permit analysis of the data
      (Signature of Parent or Guardian)

provided by my child _____ in March or April of 1976.
                   (Name of Child)

B. I _____ permit my child
      (Signature of Parent or Guardian)

_____ to complete another questionnaire for the
   (Name of Child)

study in the Spring or Fall of 1977.

If you signed either or both lines please return this letter in the enclosed envelope. No stamp is needed.

If you don't want your child in the study at all please check the square below and return the letter to us.

C. ___ I don't want my child in the study.

We hope you agree this is a worthwhile and much needed study. If you have any questions, please feel free to call me collect at 966-2017 in Chapel Hill. Thank you very much for your consideration.

Cordially,

Karl E. Bauman, Ph.D.
Study Director

KEB/bj

Enclosures

APPENDIX F
MISSING VALUES FOR SALIENCE
AND SUBJECTIVE PROBABILITY

MISSING VALUES FOR SALIENCE AND
SUBJECTIVE PROBABILITY

Some subjects did not indicate the salience and/or subjective probability for each attribute they chose. This Appendix describes the criteria used to eliminate from the analysis some cases with such incomplete information, and the method of estimating missing values for some of the subjects retained in the analysis.

The salience and subjective probability items of the questionnaire (Appendix A) are considered as eight separate sets: Round 1 salience and Round 1 subjective probability for the positive and negative attributes (4 sets), and Round 2 salience and Round 2 subjective probability for the positive and negative attributes (4 sets). Within each set there are either 26 items for the positive attributes or 28 items for the negative attributes. When the subject chose an attribute but did not indicate either its salience or subjective probability it was considered a missing value. If, for example, a subject chose the positive attribute "get high" but did not mark the corresponding salience, then that would be considered a missing value. A "completed response" was obtained when the subject completed the salience or subjective probability associated with the chosen attribute within the set. Thus, when "high" was chosen as a positive attribute and the subject responded to the corresponding salience item, that is considered a completed response.

As indicated in Chapter 4, 60 subjects who had more missing values than completed responses in one or more of the sets were eliminated from all analyses. For example, a subject who chose seven positive attributes, marked three of the corresponding salience items, and had four missing values for salience in that set was not included. Such cases were omitted because it was assumed that they had too few completed responses relative to missing values to derive satisfactory estimates for missing values.

Of the subjects retained for analysis, 251 had one or more missing values. For each of these subjects the number of completed responses was equal to or greater than the number of missing values within each set. It was assumed that removal of these cases from the analyses could produce more bias than if estimates were made of their missing values. For these cases the missing values were replaced with the average of all completed responses within the set. For example, if a subject had one missing value

TABLE F.1

Ratio of Completed Responses to Missing Values, by Set

Set	Completed Responses to Missing Values Ratios (percent of cases)		Number of Cases with Missing Values
	> 5/1	≥ 2.5/1	
Round 1			
Positive attributes			
Salience	58	95	38
Subjective probability	50	86	28
Negative attributes			
Salience	88	96	49
Subjective probability	88	92	40
Round 2			
Positive attributes			
Salience	68	93	28
Subjective probability	59	86	29
Negative attributes			
Salience	89	100	44
Subjective probability	91	100	43

Note: Since a case could have missing values in more than one set the total number of cases is 299 rather than 269 in this table.

TABLE F.2

Cases with Estimates for Missing Values and No Missing Values, by Use of Marijuana (percent of cases)

	Estimates for Missing Values	No Missing Values	Total
Rounds 1 and 2 nonusers	66.6	71.6	70.4
Round 1 nonusers, Round 2 users	19.1	16.9	17.4
Round 1 users	14.3	11.5	12.2
Total	100.0	100.0	100.0
N	251	827	1,078

Note: Chi square = 2.52, p = .28.

and four completed responses for Round 1 subjective probability related to positive attributes, the one missing value was replaced with the average of the four completed responses on Round 1 subjective probability.

Most of the 251 cases for whom these estimates were made had very few missing values: across all sets, 192 (76.5 percent) had one, 39 (15.5 percent) had two, 9 (3.6 percent) had three, 7 (3.0 percent) had four, three (1.2 percent) had five, and one (.4 percent) had more than five missing values. Since a case could have a maximum of 216 missing values (the total of positive and negative salience and subjective probability items in Rounds 1 and 2), this does not appear excessive.

Table F.1 shows by subset the ratio of completed responses to missing values. In most cases the missing values were estimated from many more completed responses than missing values.

In other analyses it was clear that missing values were distributed randomly across attributes. That is, no positive or negative consequence had a disproportionate share of missing values. As shown in Table F.2, cases with and without estimates for missing values were distributed similarly for the major subgroups of this research. Finally, all analyses in Chapter 5 were repeated without the cases with estimated values and the results were identical to those shown in that chapter.

INDEX

alcohol, 11, 15, 21-22, 123, 125

antecedent variables, 7, 8, 9, 14, 15, 32, 72-84, 88, 89-94, 95, 97, 117-20; anxiety, 8; aspiration, 91; availability, 7, 8, 78, 79; boredom, 7, 73, 114, 126; emotional stability, 7; likelihood of college, 87, 97; peer use, 7, 8, 73, 78-79, 87, 91, 95-97, 118; rebelliousness, 87, 126; religiosity, 78; Round 1, 86; sociability, 78, 91, 95; stress, 87, 122, 126; studies on, 76

Attribute Index, 54, 56, 58-59, 62, 66-70, 71, 83, 95-96, 101-4

Attribute-Salience Index 54, 56, 58-59, 67-70, 101-4

Attribute-Salience-Subjective Probability Index, 55-56, 58-59, 67-70, 101-4

Attribute-Salience-Time Index, 55-56, 58-59, 67-70, 101-4

Attribute-Subjective Probability Index, 54, 56-57, 58-62, 67-70, 79-80, 82, 86-87, 89-90, 99-104

Attribute-Subjective Probability-Time Index, 55-56, 58-59, 67-70, 101-4

Attribute-Time Index, 54, 56, 58-59, 66-71, 80-81, 91, 93-94, 101-4; Round 1, 91

Bentham, Jeremy, 11

caveats, 117-18

chi-squares, 52, 53, 58, 60

college students, 12, 14

covariance, analysis of, 99, 102

credibility gap, 121

data collection, 20, 21, 23, 25-26, 33-34, 39, 61, 106, 115, 119-20; Round 1, 33, 35, 108; Round 2, 39

data storage, 36, 38-39

demographic characteristics, 44-45, 118; age, 44-45, 91, 95, 97; parents' level of education, 44-45, 76; place of residence, 16; race, 16, 44-45, 91, 95; sex, 16, 44-45, 91

drug abuse education, studies of, 121-22

drug behavior, studies of: Jessor, 71, 82, 126; Kandel, 41, 61, 71, 82, 126; Lettieri, 71, 82, 126; Nehemkis, Macari, and Lettieri, 32

drug legislation, 122

drug use, studies of, 61, 84, 117; Albrecht and Carpenter, 13-14; Blum et al., 13; Blumenfield et al., 12; Bowden, 12; Brown et al., 12; Eells, 12; Halikas, Goodwin, and Guze, 12; Jessor, 14; Kandel, 14; Kalant and Kalant, 12-13; Lettieri, 14; Meier and Johnson, 13-14; Pomazal and Brown, 13-14; Rouse and Ewing, 14; Silberman, 13-14; Weinstein, 13-14

ABOUT THE AUTHOR

KARL E. BAUMAN received the B.A. and M.A. in Sociology
from the University of Nebraska at Lincoln, and the Ph.D. in
Sociology from Florida State University. He is Professor of
Maternal and Child Health in the School of Public Health at the
University of North Carolina at Chapel Hill. Professor Bauman's
research has been published in a wide variety of prestigious professional journals, including Demography, Social Biology, American
Journal of Public Health, Journal of Marriage and the Family, and
American Journal of Sociology. His current research focuses upon
public health policies and programs, and the application of decision-
making theories to understanding human behavior.